SECRET PLACE VISIONS

One Man's Encounter with his Creator

Volume One

By Ryker R. Kern

Illustrations by Caleb Havertape

GOLDEN BELLE PUBLISHING, LLC

73858 VALLE VISTA RD.

TWENTYNINE PALMS, CA 92277

~ i ~

ACKNOWLEDGMENT

There is one acknowledgment which must be made, that is to my precious mate and help mete, the love of my life, my beloved and best friend. She who is the joy of my heart and the "happy thought" which makes me fly. This is a tribute to her who is everything that takes my breath away. To the one who is my moon, my stars, my sunrise, and sunset. To her who is the cool breeze upon my face and the blessing of all blessings. To her who is my lover, my beautiful wife; my Belle.

There are many virtuous daughters in the world. But you, my Bride, excel them all. Every other would have thought I'd lost my mind years ago. All others would have jumped ship long ago. But not you! You bask in these visions and are one with my walks before the Lord. You are one with me. We are inseparable. We are one, like I have never seen one before.

To the woman who thinks the extraordinary should be ordinary. To the woman who thinks the whole world is crazy, but still worth our lives, and who looks at little tiny "us" and sees the power of God to alter the universe and blueprint the course of humanity. To the woman who gives her life for me daily. To her who runs to greet me at the end of my day. To her who loves to snuggle. To her who loves, loves, loves me with all her heart, mind, and soul. To the woman who encouraged me, with my fondest dreams, to dream bigger. And finally, to my mate who diligently took copious notes about these visions as if they were her own. None of these books could have been possible if you had not seen how the world needed these visions just as much as we did. Thank you, my Treasure.

Twenty-seven years and I am still so deeply in love with you.

Secret Place Visions – Volume One

By Ryker Ridge Kern – Illustrations by Caleb Havertape

Golden Belle Publishing, LLC

73858 Valle Vista Dr., Twentynine Palms, CA 92277

Printed in the United States of America

ISBN-13:-978-0692214770

DEDICATION

This book is dedicated to my King and Savior, my Lord and Sovereign God, my Truest and Dearest Friend; the Lord Jesus Christ, His Holy Spirit, and His Father. To You, who first loved me and sought me. To You, who led me by the way that I should go, despite all my complaining, groaning, and pleadings. To You who never let me settle for where I would have been satisfied. To You, who kicked me in the posterior throughout the course of my journey; in order to keep me digging still deeper for Truth. You have my deepest gratitude for daily walking with me in the cool of the morning, listening to me, and confiding in me. To hear a single word from You, to see Your approach, or to receive a warm embrace from the omnipotent Creator of the universe, this would be the most extraordinary experience imaginable for any human being. Yet, how do I measure what it means to walk with You every day? What does it mean that Your voice is as familiar to me as my own wife or children's? All this is beyond words. Thank You, Lord. And for when I take Your familiarity for granted, please excuse me for not remembering how precious Your voice and the sight of Your face is. You are so much more than a familiar friend. You are, and always will be, my Lord and Master. Thank you for preparing this secret place for me, and meeting me there. You are the air I breathe. Every heartbeat proclaims Your exceeding goodness upon this mere mortal whom You have seated at Your table. Thank You, Father.

TABLE OF CONTENTS

LIST OF ILLUSTRATIONS

INTRODUCTION

Prequels and Sequels

Of all the places to begin writing a book, this chapter of my personal walk with the Lord seems the most awkward to begin with. It brings to mind many movie series. That is, those which leave one asking "Now, is this a prequel, sequel, or somewhere in the middle?" Why can't they just write these stories in order, and do us all a small favor?

That being said, it is odd then that this first book of mine should also begin somewhere in the middle. My wife asked the other day, "Why begin writing here?" My answer? "Sweetheart, everything God has taught me is rooted in my relationship with Him. It is the whole point of everything He has planted in my heart. In order to pass His lessons to others, these visions are the very best means to accomplish that. They are my story." So often, in mentoring others, this is the central truth to what each of us has to offer others. Our story. "This is what Jesus did in my life, and He wants to do great things in yours as well." A blind man healed by Jesus was brought before the know-it-all-religious-leaders of his day and asked, "Who is this man who healed you?" His reply?

He answered and said, "Whether He be a sinner or no, I know not: one thing I know, that, whereas I was blind, now I see." Then said they to him again, "What did He to thee? How opened He thine eyes?" He answered them, "I have told you already, and ye did not hear: wherefore would ye hear it again? will ye also be His disciples?" Then they reviled him, and said, "Thou art His disciple; but we are Moses' disciples. We know that God spake unto Moses: as for this Fellow we know not from whence He is." The man answered and said unto them, "Why herein is a marvelous thing, that ye know not from whence He is, and yet He hath opened mine eyes. Now we know that God heareth not sinners: but if any man be a worshipper of God, and doeth His will, him He heareth. Since the world began was it not heard that any man opened the eyes of one that was born blind? If this man were not of God, He could do nothing. They answered and said unto him, Thou wast altogether born in sins, and dost thou teach us? And they cast him out."

John. 9:25-34 (KJV)

We all have a story to share about Jesus, and this is mine. All that is intended, with this book, is to share these experiences and pass on the lessons that accompany them. If they were common experiences, there would be no point, and certainly hold little interest. However, as you will see, these personal encounters are unique and they reveal something incredibly significant about our God. What He desires to share with each of us, compels the writing down of these moments.

Personal Encounters

There is no escaping the fact that these encounters are very personal in nature. They were intended for me, and not meant to reveal any great theological truth. They are simply what they are. The sharing of them is merely a window one can look through to see how God desires to connect with and bless us.

So, "If they are personal, why publish them?" Most importantly: because He said to. These experiences are not meant to serve as a model for anyone. Nor, is it suggested or implied that anything will be found which is not already revealed through Scripture. For those that worship both in Spirit and Truth though, wisdom and understanding will be your reward. What is God's reward in this project? What He desires the most; intimacy with you.

There are many things that one should be able to take away from this reading. First, readers should be able to see numerous and meaningful correlations between these experiences and theirs. While the secret place revealed here is personal, it is also clearly representative of the church (body) at large. Hopefully, you will be able to obtain a tangible glimpse of what is possible in your own relationship with God.

The True Nature of Visions

Visions are wonderful. They are easy to grow to love and enjoy deeply. They are however, fluid and not absolute in their nature. Independently, they are not the Word of God, nor are they held up to the same standard of absolute. No matter how long a person may have been walking in the Spirit, not letting "self" get mixed up in our interpretation and assimilation of what we hear or see is always difficult. Don't be fooled though, the Word of God (The Bible) itself is just as vulnerable to "self." It is very difficult for all humans, and even impossible for some, to read and understand God's Word (the Bible) without "self" coloring and twisting their understanding of it. It is very important to keep in mind that only God's Word is absolute, not our understanding of it. Nor do our words about His Word carry the same authority.

This does not mean visions and dreams are insignificant or unnecessary. As for me and my wife, who have tested the Spirit (as outlined in the Scripture) and found Him above reproach, we have come to trust and act upon God's voice and these visions daily. We always hold God's Word in our right hand and the Spirit in the left, as all true worshippers of God do. It is **ONLY** in the act of worshipping God both in Spirit and Truth that anyone can know what they know is true. An individual simply cannot worship God in Truth, without also worshiping Him in Spirit.

The Bible tells us that in the last days "And it shall come to pass afterward, *that* I will pour out my spirit upon all flesh; and your sons and your daughters shall prophesy, your old men shall dream dreams, your young men shall see visions" (Joel 2:28 & Acts 2:17) Here we see that God has spoken of this day, what is there then left to debate?

"...I will utter things which have been kept secret from the foundation of the world."   **Matthew 13:35 (KJV)**

Is This Secret Place Real?

Is this secret place real? Well, that depends on the nature of the question. First and foremost, nearly everything in the following visions are metaphors for both the natural and spiritual life. If the question is: "Can this place be found on the earth? Could a person drive to it and touch it with their hands? This seems seriously doubtful. Could this scene be found somewhere in Heaven? That is unknown, but would not be surprising in the least. Can other people visit this secret place? Actually, yes. In spirit, they already have.

What is this place then? This is what is known so far: it is a place God prepared for me to meet Him. Here in our secret place, He can teach me, walk with me, heal me, encourage me, and restore me. It is a spiritual place of refuge where I can go at will, to be with my Lord. It is a place to get my questions answered. It is a place to go for physical and emotional healing. It is a place to see things that cannot be seen with natural eyes. It is a place to hear things that cannot be heard with natural ears. It is a place to enjoy each other's company. And, the Lord Jesus tells me He has such a place for every person who seeks it with all their heart and all due perseverance. Furthermore, as He did with me, He will do it in a personal way that meets every person where they are.

How The Visions Come

Now, a small word regarding how these visions come: Initially, some of the visions were merely dreams like any other dream one might have while sleeping. In a short time though, these visions took on a life of their own. Visions are not re-occurring dreams. Re-occurring dreams are still just dreams. A vision however, can occur spontaneously even while awake. I have found that after I grew used to them, they could also be consciously initiated at will. Once initiated though, they always take off to where God wills they go. Though access might be by will, the vision itself it always directed outside of one's will. It is never known beforehand where they go, nor where they will end up.

During most, but not all, the mind is physically conscious (not asleep). However, it would be accurate to say there is a willful detachment from the natural environment. The spirit is operating solo during those encounters. The body is in submission and agreeably steps aside to rest. Again, learning to walk in the Spirit in this manner did not happen overnight. There was a significant process of seeking, pressing in to a relationship with God, and growing in maturity. As much as it would be great to talk about that process now, it will nevertheless have to wait for a later book. Bear in mind, we will get to the prequel of these stories at another time.

Now, to the big question everyone wants to know:

What Does Jesus Look Like?

Oddly enough, it was quite some time before I actually started paying attention to His features, as one would any other person. Actually, it was not until a close friend asked about His features that it occurred to me to describe Him. In the Spirit, it seemed far more natural to feel His presence than to see His presence (with eyes). Don't misunderstand, it was not as if He lacked visual appearance or the substance of matter. That's not it at all.

Rather, it simply did not occur to me to note His physical features; as one does when assessing people in the natural world. When attempts were eventually made to focus on His features, it felt unnatural to do so. It took several visions of purposely focusing on Him, before His physical features finally became clear. Once successful though, it became easy and eventually even natural to see Him. By that time, seeing every nuance of His expressions became as familiar to me as my own wife's.

This process is understandable, as our spirit simply has no regard for the exterior of a person. Our spirit only feels (senses) the other person's spirit. The spirit has no more knowledge, nor sense of the flesh, than the flesh does the world of the spirit. Strange as it may seem, assessing a person spiritually is a considerably more reliable means of knowing them than recognizing their natural features. It's not that there is no visible exterior, it's just that the spirit is no more interested in the outside of a person, than the natural man is interested in the inside of a person.

Here is how I would describe Him. He appears to be in His mid-thirties. He is about 5'10" and weighs about 175lbs. His hair is a light brown, straight, and it is only long enough to go over his collar. He has a short, well groomed beard and mustache. In every situation so far He has appeared to me in dress appropriate for a warrior prince. Despite this appearance, I have never actually seen Him carrying a sword or other weapon during any of the encounters so far, with two exceptions. Much later, in another volume, there will be some visions described where He is sparring with me in swordplay. However, He requests a sword from an angel at the time, rather than carrying one. And even then, He only does so to train me. Then on another occasion, He drew a sword and fought off a hoard of demons (not a secret place vision). At that time, He did so to protect me when I had fallen from exhaustion in a battle. It is not until much later in these visions that I learn the significance of this observation.

"The LORD is a Man of War: The LORD is His name."   **Exodus 15:3 (KJV)**

"And it came to pass, when Joshua was by Jericho, that he lifted up his eyes and looked, and, behold, there stood a man (Jesus) **over against him <u>with His sword drawn in His hand</u>: and Joshua went unto Him, and said unto Him, 'Art Thou for us, or for our adversaries?' And He said, 'Nay; but as Captain of the Host of the LORD am I now come.' And Joshua fell on his face to the earth, <u>and did worship</u>,** (First indication that it was Jesus and not an angel. We know that angels will not permit worship of them) **and said unto Him, 'What saith my Lord unto His servant?' And the Captain of the LORD'S Host said unto Joshua, <u>'Loose thy shoe from off thy foot; for the place whereon thou standest is holy</u>.'** (Reminiscent of God appearing to Moses. Angelic appearances do not make the ground holy. Removing his shoes was another act of worship) **And Joshua did so."**   **Joshua 5:13-15 (KJV)**

"And I saw Heaven opened, and behold a white horse; and He that sat upon him was called Faithful and True, and in righteousness <u>He doth judge and make war</u>. His eyes were as a flame of fire, and on His head were many crowns; and He had a name written, that no man knew, but He Himself. And He was clothed with a vesture dipped in blood: and <u>His name is called The Word of God</u>. And the armies which were in Heaven followed Him upon white horses, clothed in fine linen, white and clean. <u>And out of His mouth goeth a sharp sword</u>, that with it He should smite the nations: and He shall rule them with a rod of iron: and He treadeth the winepress of the fierceness and wrath of Almighty God. And He hath on His vesture and on His thigh a name written, KING OF KINGS, AND LORD OF LORDS."   **Rev. 19:11-16 (KJV)**

In all these encounters (visions) He gives off the air of Brotherhood, more than one of Lordship, as He relates to me. He always makes direct eye contact and leans into connecting with me. It's hard to describe how it feels in His presence. Our connecting is very easy. It's natural and not intimidating, with some exceptions. He feels like an older Brother in many respects. Imagine having a much older brother who leaves home and comes back in a U.S. Marine uniform. Imagine yourself being about ten years old and looking up to Him. If you can do that, you will begin to imagine what it might feel like to be with Him. I look up to and admire Him. He is my whole world. He looks at me and loves me as His little brother whom He loves to teach, to bless, to protect, and to give good things too. This may not be exactly what it is, but that is sort of what it feels like if I were asked to describe it in any amount of detail.

My Words about His Words

Regarding interpretations: Except in the case of quotations of scripture, there is no intention to make any "Thus Saith the Lord" statements. These are personal visions, and my own personal interpretations of them. Even my use of Scripture, as it should be with any other teacher of Scripture, ought to be considered only my opinion. That is, unless otherwise proven by diligent study and the Holy Spirit's revelation. This being said, there is a reason so much Scripture is woven into this book. And, there are substantial reasons for my opinions expressed herein. On the other hand, the reader is just as obligated to reconcile their own opinions about these matters with the Scriptures, as I am.

Great care has been taken to demonstrate the firm foundation for the statements made in this book. My personal belief system, the one which frames the support for this trustworthy faith in our Lord, has come at some great expense to me and my family. It is not a philosophy, nor recreational intellectual banter. My life, my family's' daily lives, and our eternity all weigh in on the truth of this belief system. It is no small matter. Our life literally depends on upon what I believe to be right, actually is RIGHT !!! With so much at stake, one simply cannot afford to be wrong. This fact is as true for the reader as the writer, whether you realize it or not.

The strongest recommendation possible is extended to the reader to follow the first century Berean's example. Dig into God's Word and see if what is said herein, is so. We are all called to rightly divide the Word of God. (If it can be rightly divided, it stands to reason that it can also be wrongly divided.) Remember, it is so very easy to fall on the wrong side of right without even knowing it. We should never believe everything we think. It is always recommended we question everything, especially ourselves. There has to be an absolute basis for our belief system. It is imperative that we go beyond the attitude of, "this is what I was taught," or "I'm just not comfortable with that." The only question which matters is this; "Is it true or not?" Anything outside of this is an irrational pseudo-religious belief system that has no more legitimacy than believing the moon is made of cheese. Simply believing, with all your heart, cannot make a lie true.

Regarding personal notes inserted into Scriptures within this book: While addressing Scriptures, for simplification purposes, there are personal notes set apart within the Scriptures by parenthesis. These are meant merely to help the reader see what the writer sees. However, these notes are not to be taken as Scripture. They are just my words about His Words.

On the matter of conscious, my responsibility for the potential of leading people astray is taken very seriously. There ARE times when it becomes necessary to make divine declarations from the Lord. At such moments it is essential that people are able to trust the words of the man of God and treat them with all seriousness. This is difficult to do if the pastor or teacher has abused his influence and given divine authority to his own personal words.

Often when making a spiritual statement to my wife, she will ask "Did God say that?" If I said He did, she would believe me. She would believe me because she trusts me. The reason she trusts me is because I am careful to always to distinguish my thoughts from His. If she asks and I didn't hear it straight from Him, I will say, "No, it was my own thought." I need her to be able to trust me when it's really important. When I say, "this is from the Lord", she obeys. Therefore, I NEVER abuse that trust. Many spiritual leaders may. But, I DO NOT.

Eyes to See, and Ears to Hear

And, finally, to those blessed of God who have not seen, and yet believe... To those who see miracles everywhere they go... To those whose heart is open to God wherever He may appear.... To those who know their God makes promises so He can keep them, To those who know their God to be a good, loving, personal God, and an intimate friend.... To those who know Him as their Groom...To you who long for His coming as a Bride does.... If these visions edify you in any way, take them, they are yours! You are the reason they were written. To all, greetings and God's blessings as you embark upon this adventure with me.

Ryker Ridge Kern

PSALM 91

1 He that dwelleth in the "Secret Place" of the most High shall abide under the shadow of the Almighty.

Those who dwell in Zion (the Kingdom of Heaven) shall be protected by the Almighty God 24/7

2 I will say of the LORD, He is my refuge and my fortress: my God; in Him will I trust.

That person will declare that God is His absolute protector. In His omnipotence, that man will trust without reservation.

3 Surely He shall deliver thee from the snare of the fowler, and from the noisome pestilence.

It is certain (guaranteed) that God will deliver him from all the traps that are laid for him. And from the deadly diseases that ravage the land.

4 He shall cover thee with His feathers, and under His wings shalt thou trust: His truth shall be thy shield and buckler.

He will cover that person the way a hen covers her brood. And he will trust Him the way they trust her, because He is worthy of trust. The Word of God will be an impenetrable barrier against all attacks.

5 Thou shalt not be afraid for the terror by night; nor for the arrow that flieth by day;

He will never be afraid of the undetectable things that kill people in the darkness, nor of the things that kill others in the open light of day.

6 Nor for the pestilence that walketh in darkness; nor for the destruction that wasteth at noonday.

Nor will he ever be afraid of unknown disease that overtakes others without them knowing about it until it's too late. Nor will he be afraid of those that destroy people out in the open.

7 A thousand shall fall at thy side, and ten thousand at thy right hand; but it shall not come nigh thee.

While he may witness a thousand people die at his side due to catastrophes, and even when he sees ten thousand people destroyed at his right hand....none of these things will come near him who dwells in Zion (the sheltered place of the most High).

8 Only with thine eyes shalt thou behold and see the reward of the wicked.

Only with his eyes will that man witness the destruction of his brothers and sisters who have an unbelieving heart. The destruction will not visit him, nor anything that is his.

9 Because thou hast made the LORD, which is my refuge, even the most High, thy habitation;

And here is why these things will not come anywhere near such a man. Because He has made the Lord God of all Creation his hiding place and He lives there with Him day and night.

10 There shall no evil befall thee, neither shall any plague come nigh thy dwelling.

No bad thing will fall upon this man and no sickness will come near his home and those he loves.

11 For he shall give his angels charge over thee, to keep thee in all thy ways.

Because God has given His warring angels the charge of protecting him and they will guard him everywhere He goes.

12 They shall bear thee up in their hands, lest thou dash thy foot against a stone.

They will carry him in their hands watching over him so intently that he should not even be concerned with stubbing his toe against a rock, much less the destruction that come upon those who do not believe these words with their whole heart.

13 Thou shalt tread upon the lion and adder: the young lion and the dragon shalt thou trample under feet.

That man will walk confidently over everything that normally harms or kills other people. He will walk over them as if they were nothing. Because, God's promises are more certain than the threats of anything He created.

14 Because he hath set his love upon Me, therefore will I deliver him: I will set him on high, because he hath known My Name.

God says with His own mouth that because this man has set his love upon Me, I WILL DELIVER HIM; I WILL EXALT HIM BEFORE ALL OTHER PEOPLE, because that man knows Me.

15 He shall call upon Me, and I will answer him: I will be with him in trouble; I will deliver him, and honor him.

Furthermore, when that man calls out to Me for help, I WILL ANSWER HIM: I WILL BE WITH HIM THROUGH ALL HIS TROUBLES, I WILL DELIVER HIM FROM THOSE TROUBLES, AND I WILL HONOR HIM BEFORE ALL OTHER PEOPLE ON THE EARTH.

16 With long life will I satisfy him, and shew him My salvation

His promise is this; that He WILL GIVE THAT MAN A LONG LIFE. A long life that will end only when that man is satisfied, and then...God will Show that man the Heaven He prepared for him. That man will walk confidently over everything that normally harms or kills other people. He will walk over them as if they were nothing. Because, God's promises are more certain than the threats of anything He created.

Secret Place

Visions

One Man's Encounter with his Creator

Volume One

By Ryker R. Kern

Illustrations by Caleb Havertape

By Caleb Havertape

Chapter One

BREAKING TRAIL WITH JESUS

While sleeping one night, I heard the Lord say "Follow me, I want to show you something." Upon opening my eyes, I found myself following Jesus through dense underbrush in a thickly wooded forest. As I was behind Him, His face was not visible to me, but I knew it was Him. This sort of thing had never happened to me before, so it was somewhat startling to find myself here. Oddly enough though, it felt natural and familiar. So, I continued on with little concern. Dry branches and leaves could be heard snapping under our feet. Even the brush of a limb across my face could be felt.

There was this distinct impression we were in an area near my hometown. This may have been why it seemed familiar to me. The time of year felt like September. The air was cool, the wind was blowing slightly, the leaves on the trees had the first signs of turning to their fall colors, and I was wearing my Carhardt jacket. He was wearing what appeared to be a leather outfit common to a warrior prince of the medieval period.

For the moment, we were in the process of struggling to get through all the brush and other vegetation before us. It was arduous work as we moved aside limbs, stepped over fallen logs, and pulled ourselves through tangles of vines and brambles. We had been diligently employed in this manner for about fifteen minutes, when He suddenly took a change in direction to the left. Despite the lack of any evidence of a trail, He clearly knew where He was going. We only went on for a few more minutes, when stopping abruptly, and turning to face me for the first time, He motioned for me to come up alongside Him.

Stepping up alongside Him into an opening in the vegetation, I shook the leaves and small limbs off my jacket. The trees and overhanging branches blocked out much of the sun, so it was shaded where we stood. Apparently, we had arrived at what He wanted to show me. However, what was to be seen was not immediately evident.

Looking to where He was pointing, I beheld beams of sunlight which were streaming in and falling upon some kind of ancient structure. It was nearly obscured from sight under leafy vines and other vegetation that had overtaken it many years ago. Studying what could be seen of the structure, I realized it was a white country chapel with a steeple and two big front doors. It appeared to have been abandoned for a very long, long time. Intrigued by the sight, I shifted my position to get a better look. After my eyes adjusted to the variations in the streaming light coming through the overhead canopy of trees, it was easier to see the peeling paint, rotted wood, and broken windows.

We only paused there for a few moments. It was on the tip of my tongue to ask Him about it. Unfortunately though, He started off toward the door before I got the chance to speak. Walking up the steps, He moved some vines aside and reached through them to open the left hand door. The hinges creaked as He pushed firmly on it. A pile of leaves and dust also plowed up behind the door as He opened it. This made the task even more difficult. Ducking under the vines, He entered and held them aside so I might step inside as well.

A thick coat of dust on the hardwood floors was the first thing to catch my attention. There were no pews or pulpit, only open space. Windows coated with dust, allowed only a scattered haze of light in. "Lord, what is this place?!" I asked. Walking to the center, He spun around and spread His arms wide. He said, "This is your secret place. In it, you will find stored everything you will ever need. You may come here anytime you desire. It belongs to you. It's yours!"

Clearly this was a significant vision. To be quite honest though, I can't say I was that impressed with the gift. I mean talk about your fixer-uppers. This place was a wreck. I'm glad I did not comment though, due to the embarrassing revelation to follow. He would explain that this place, was actually me. It was my life that was the wreck. This place, my secret place, was a reflection of my spiritual condition.

Perceiving my lack of enthusiasm, He motioned toward something I'd not yet taken notice of. All four walls were lined with many tall, narrow, ornate closets. They reminded me of Colonial or Victorian era wardrobes. (later He would refer to them as "Enclaves".) They were about six feet tall, three feet wide, two feet deep, and had gable roofs. I wondered what was in them. Knowing my thoughts, He answered,

BY CALEB HAVERTAPE

"Anything you will ever want or need is stored in these. Everything in them is available for the taking: healing, provision, resources, wisdom, information, understanding… whatever you may want or need."

We walked up to one to get a better look, but didn't open it at the time. However, I did assure Him I would return after considering what He had shown me. At that, the vision ended abruptly. Upon opening my eyes, I woke my wife and shared with her what had happened.

"Know ye not that ye are the Temple of God, and that the Spirit of God dwelleth in you?" 1 Corinthians 3:16 (KJV)

By Caleb Havertape

PERSONAL COMMENTARY

The Path

The non-existent path we took, as I learned later, was the original abandoned road to the Chapel. Nature just did what nature does. The road represented the path to Truth and understanding. As with any path which ceases to be traveled, the natural world simply overtook and buried it in obscurity. Likewise, if we fail to travel this path regularly; the natural world will always do what the natural world does; take over and blind us to the Truth. Without Jesus guiding me, my secret place would still be a secret. I simply did not know what I did not know. It is therefore not surprising to me that the entire church body of our day has wandered so far from the Truth.

The Chapel

The Chapel itself represented me and the condition of my soul. It represented how long God's blessings had been available, but unaccessed. It represented the fact that I had never truly trusted, nor sought Him for all He had freely given me. It spoke of how long I had existed and moved in accordance with my own understanding, and resources. I also came to understand that this secret place also represented the church body at large.

One other thing should be mentioned for observation sake. God never seemed to take much note of the condition of my secret place. He always seemed to enjoy it just as much in its fallen state, as He did in its restored state. Oddly, it often appeared as if He took no notice of my condition at all. He appeared to enjoy my company no matter what. On the other hand, I was deeply affected by the condition of the building, especially once the true nature of it became clear. In fact, I was looking in a mirror. And I was ashamed.

THE ENCLAVES

BY CALEB HAVERTAPE

Chapter Two

THE ENCLAVES

March 24, 2010 – My Forty Seventh Birthday

It was about four months later when this second vision occurred. On that particular night, my wife, Belle, and I were talking about the first vision. During our conversation she asked, "So, what would you want to get from your secret place when you get to go back?" Unfortunately, there was not a good answer for her. At the time, what was available was incomprehensible. The next day, the question dominated my mind, "What to ask for?"

For many years now, the wee hours of the morning (2 a.m.) are usually the time when God wakes me. It is both an endearing and irritating habit He has. However, it is important to Him in order to get our quality time together (which, by the way, is His primary love language). It's the time for me to ask questions, and in turn listen to what is on His mind.

This personal experience, of hearing God's voice on a regular basis, began for me while our family was living in the Montana wilderness. Back then it was necessary, during the night, to get up every two hours in order to stoke the fire in the wood stove. Sitting up for an hour or two, bundled in blankets during the middle of the night, was common. It was easy during those times to stare into the fireplace and get totally lost in the Spirit. Sleep has never been that big a deal anyway. It was far more enjoyable just listening to the Lord talk on and on about things.

For our family, those were tough days. Rarely were we able to get the inside temperature of our home above 39 degrees that first winter. We had no electricity, and our water (that came off the mountain from a spring) would be frozen solid for 3-4 months at a time. Nevertheless, it was during those harsh times when God spoke to me more than He ever had before. In reflection, it is easy to understand why. In the solitude of our misery, in the silence of poverty, He had our undivided attention. There were no distractions; the wilderness offered a life free of busyness, and all forms of electronic entertainment. It was us, the elements, and our God.

Now, because we live in the Southern California desert, even the outside temperature rarely gets as cold as the indoor temperature during those frosty days. We are now able to heat our whole home with a couple small space heaters. It's the most wonderful thing! Nevertheless, early morning is still when God chooses to wake me. And so, it has continued ever since.

"O God, Thou art my God; early will I seek Thee: my soul thirsteth for Thee, my flesh longeth for Thee in a dry and thirsty land, where no water is (such as here in the Mojave Desert)**." Psalm 63:1 (KJV)**

"I love them that love Me; and those that seek Me early Shall find Me."

Psalm 8:17 (KJV)

"With my soul have I desired Thee in the night; yea, with my spirit within me will I seek Thee early:" Isaiah 26:9 (KJV)

"Seek ye the Lord while He may be found, call ye upon Him while He is near." Isaiah 55:6 (KJV)

"Hearken unto the voice of my cry, my King, and my God: for unto Thee will I pray. My voice shalt Thou hear in the morning, O LORD; in the morning will I direct my prayer unto Thee, and will look up." Psalm 5:2-3 (KJV)

"I will bless the LORD, Who hath given me counsel: my reins also instruct me in the night seasons." Psalm 16:7 (KJV)

On the night of this vision, I was sitting on the sofa in our darkened living room. At the moment my stomach was experiencing severe pain, the result of gastric reflux. It had been attacking unabated for many years. So, this night pain was common to me. He had said to come back anytime for healing. The expectation was that it would happen spontaneously, as it had before. But it had never happened that I should find myself in those familiar woods again. I began wondering though. Was it possible to return, by an act of will, as He had said?

With this question in mind, I purposefully began imagining myself on the same path we had taken before. It was difficult to find the way. Remembering exactly where we had gone was a bit challenging. However, while picking my way along the path, certain things did start to look familiar. In particular, there was this large oak tree where He had turned to the left last time. The moment the tree came into view, the vision "took over." That is, it began to unfold spontaneously, as it had months before.

As before, the crackling of the dry limbs under foot, and the wind gently blowing through the trees was clearly audible. After struggling through the brush a little further, I finally stumbled into the clearing. Shaking the limbs and leaves off my jacket, I looked up and was surprised to find that the little lost chapel in the woods appeared to be in considerably worse condition than before. It was almost as if another hundred years had passed since the last visit! Most noticeable was that the steeple had fallen off the roof, apparently the result of its rotted condition and a windstorm. It was now lying on the ground, upside down near the left wall. The chapel was also overtaken by a great deal more vegetation, and some of the windows were broken as well! A deep sense of shame, for not coming back sooner, swept in like a cold wind.

Apprehensively approaching the chapel, I stepped up toward the front door. At that moment, Jesus suddenly appeared in the doorway. Behaving as if the last visit were only yesterday and as if nothing had changed, He motioned with His arm and said "Come on in!" When He pushed the vines away and opened the big doors, I could see leaves and twigs scattered everywhere on the floor.

Once inside, gaping holes in the roof also became apparent. This explained the debris that had blown all over the floor. The enclaves were covered under a heavy coat of dust, leaves, and cobwebs. Interrupting my amazement, without appearing to take note of the damage Himself, He asked "What would you like first?" Hesitantly, I replied "If it's true I can have anything, then a new digestive system would sure be nice.

"That's in this one over here," He said, while motioning for me to follow. "Do you really want this?" He asked as we stepped up to one of the enclaves. "Yes Lord," I replied. "Then go ahead and open the door," He said. When I did so, a brilliant white light flooded from the enclave. He then told me to lie down. "On the dirty floor?", I thought, but complied with His instruction anyway. Sweeping away the dust and accumulation, I situated myself as comfortable as possible on the floor. Turning toward the enclave, He reached in and withdrew what He needed. Kneeling down beside me, He laid something on my body. Its mass and shape were indiscernible as it was cloaked in a brilliant white light. Leaning back, He watched as the light seemed to dissolve into my abdomen and disappear from sight.

"Anything else you would like?" He asked. Sitting up, I noticed I suddenly felt pretty good. "Maybe not to be attacked by frequent headaches anymore," I answered. Taking my hand and helping me to my feet, He pointed to an enclave in the left front corner and said, "You will find what you are looking for over there." Feeling a bit overwhelmed by all this, I asked to come for that one later. He seemed a bit confused and disappointed by this request, but received my promise to return as soon as possible. "And next time I will come with intention to fix up the place," I told Him. "Good, I'll help you," He said with a smile. He then suggested that it might be a good idea to begin by clearing the trail down here. He also mentioned that I should bring my small chainsaw, a machete, and loppers (pruning tool for cutting limbs). With that, the second vision ended.

The very next morning, the Lord instructed me go outside and declare my stomach healed. Upon arriving at work, out of habit, I reached over to grab some antacid capsules. Before this day, it was necessary to take them every few hours to keep my stomach settled. Holding them in my hand, I paused for a moment and asked myself what I was doing. "I was healed last night and will no longer need these," I reminded myself. Then the Lord spoke up and asked, "Do you want this healing or not?" Quickly dropping them as if they were hot potatoes, I went to work. This was the last time they were ever touched, until they got thrown away several weeks later.

THE ENCLAVES

BY CALEB HAVERTAPE

PERSONAL COMMENTARY

Above all, this vision proved returning to my newly acquired "Secret Place" by an act of the will was possible! Furthermore, it proved by pressing in, His presence could be accessed. This was not a new truth to me. It was how I learned to hear His voice in the first place. Years before, when our first two children were young and our family was in need of answers, I purposed to not rest until I could hear Him. His Word is clear. **"My sheep hear My voice" John 10:27**. He does not withhold any good thing from His children, especially Himself.

At that time, we owned a home in central Washington state with a one acre orchard. It was always enjoyable walking among the trees while praying. But then I decided to take it a step further. We were looking for God to fulfill His Word to us, and be our Deliverer in especially hard times. We were desperate for answers and had not heard God's voice for about five years. We needed break through, It was clear that additional spiritual action had to be taken.

With my Bible in hand one night, I walked to the end of our driveway. Once there, I told the Lord that I was sick and tired of the silence and that He was going to talk to me whether He liked it or not. "You can conceal yourself all you want Lord, but you cannot hide yourself from me," I declared, "You are going to talk to me, and here is why." Holding my Bible up in the air, I went on, "Because you have promised me you would manifest yourself to me! I am not making it up, its right here in your Bible." With that I started reading His own promises back to Him.

After a few moments of that, I said "Here is what I am going to do. Every day, come rain or shine, I am going to walk the entire perimeter of our property, from marker to marker, reading Your promises to You out loud. On Sundays, we will do this walk seven times. At the end of each walk, I will stand in the middle of the orchard for ten minutes waiting for You to say something." With that, off I went for the first walk. A little over two years later, I was **still** walking our property line daily reading His promises to a wall of silence.

Then suddenly one day, mid-way between the first and second property markers and mid-sentence where I was reading in Isaiah, something happened. His voice came out of nowhere and began reading the passage to me. It stunned me so much that I stopped walking and looked around for where the voice was coming from.. At first, I had no idea what was going on. Despite my bewilderment, He just continued reading. Then His Spirit came down on me, and I fell on my face weeping. Laying there in the grass with great emotion, I could still hear Him reading to me. **FINALLY,** God had spoken to me. It was about ten minutes before I could pull myself together well enough to stand. After that, every time I went out to read…He would read to me. Still the only time He spoke to me was when I was reading His promises to Him. So, I read a lot in the days to follow!

Just this morning I found a picture with a caption and shared it with my wife. In the picture was a five year old girl with no hands trying to draw a picture with her teeth. The caption read, "Don't quit until you have tried." So many people sum up their whole effort to seek God with these words, "I tried praying once; and it didn't work." Try praying every day for two years, with no results!

In this second vision, it also became evident how important it was to enter into His presence sooner and much more frequently. It clearly demonstrated that the passage of time, without the care to access His presence, can be detrimental to one's personal well-being. It is also observable how a brief period of time (four months) in the natural, was represented as considerable in the spiritual (years). It is notable that a great deal of progress can be lost in a very brief amount of time.

Interestingly, it appeared as if Jesus is always fine whether we enjoy His benefits or not. It stands to reason that it is only us, and those who depend upon us, who suffer from our complacency and unbelief. There is no lack within Him when we rob ourselves of His benefits! And it also became clear that there really was healing in the enclaves, as He had promised. The vision demonstrated that healing is easy for those who believe and receive it without reservation. It is proof that healing is just not complicated.

Not surprisingly, the most disappointing personal observation was my hesitation in receiving the second healing. How dismayed I was to find that it was difficult to believe without doubting! To my defense, these encounters were still so new for me. One would have to admit, these visions were asking a great deal more faith than most would be prepared to believe. And, it seemed to me at the time that believing for the first healing was the most important thing to secure. In my mind, there was no hurry.

This second vision established the fact that not only was it possible to return, but doing so was going to become a regular thing. Therefore, my confidence level was considerably higher in believing for a return visit, than it was to believe for two great healing miracles at once. It seemed "reasonable" to expect that there would be plenty of opportunity to receive the second healing. The reality though, is that the second healing was just as available to me right then as the first was. And, although my capacity to receive it was limited, Jesus wanted me to have it on this visit.

So, at this particular time and for all practical purposes, I was in a great deal of needless pain. If there had been enough belief within me during the first vision to simply ask for it, I wouldn't have had to continue to suffer. Had there been greater understanding on my part, it wouldn't have been a problem to ask for what was needed immediately. Nevertheless, this trial moved me to make the choice to believe from then on and rebuild in accordance with His Word. It is never too late to access God's promises. But sooner sure beats later, unless one enjoys misery.

And finally, through this vision it became clear that restoring this chapel would become a graphic spiritual means of restoring me in the natural as well. So, what about the symbolic metaphors in this vision? Let's talk about what can be learned from the metaphors in this vision.

Abandoned Chapel

The little chapel, and its long abandoned state, is a clear representation of the years of my life spent without access to what God had prepared for me. Let me be clear though. Ever since being a boy, I have sought the Lord with all my heart and diligently studied His Word with a voracious appetite. There has never been a time in my life where I turned away from trying to apprehend God with a passion. Furthermore, I have been in ministry nearly my whole life; pastoring, teaching, discipling, and serving in evangelism; as well as any other need that could be filled. I took my family to church every week, and we homeschooled our children in the Word.

This vision however, clearly illustrated my own personal negligence in seeking God for His great promises (blessings). It effectively demonstrated that His blessings had always been available to me, but they were not evident in my life. Unfortunately, in my day-to-day walk with Him, His benefits had long been forgotten and buried under truckloads of disappointment, doubt, and unbelief.

(David's spirit encouraging his soul to not forget what I forgot.) **"Bless the Lord, O my soul, and forget not ALL HIS BENEFITS; Who forgiveth ALL thine iniquities, who healeth ALL they diseases; Who REDEEMETH thy life from destruction; who CROWNETH thee with lovingkindness and tender mercies; Who SATISFIETH thy mouth with GOOD THINGS; so that THY YOUTH IS RENEWED like the eagle's. The Lord executeth righteousness and judgment for ALL that are oppressed." Psalm 103:2-6 (KJV)**

What are Abandoned Blessings?

To answer this question, one would have to go the BEGINNING. That is, to the time everything was created. One must start with the ULTIMATE QUESTION. Despite what people may say, the ultimate question is not HOW we got here. That is no big news flash. The ultimate question is the meaning of life; "WHY are we here?" So, what is the answer to the Ultimate Question of Life, the Universe, and Everything that exists?

The meaning to all life, and all matter which exists, is contained within a single statement: "God created all existence for the express purpose of enjoying the companionship of a mate; and having done so, to express His affection for His mate through that which He made for her." All existence owes its existence to this fact. God is preparing a Bride for Himself. Everything that has existed facilitates this ultimate outcome.

God is Love. This statement is no different than saying "Ryker is Human." Love is as much a state of being for God, as being human is for me. Though I may know how to love, it is not my state of being. For God, it is. It defines Him as much as being human defines me.

As disappointing as the following statement may be to our big dog, Sitka, it is still true: Just because our dog lives in our house, eats our food, is part of our family, and is convinced he is human, it does not make him human. In the same manner, I have love and share love, but God IS Love. It is the total nature of His state of being and existence as an individual. It defines Him. One may accurately refer to me as a human. One may also refer to God accurately as Love. Therefore anything we may know or understand about love, which is able be truly defined as such, owes itself to our model...God. For God <u>IS</u> Love.... He is our Lover.

Some may feel uncomfortable with the word – Lover. But God wrote the Song of Solomon, in which He describes Himself as an impassioned Lover seeking His soul mate. I am not talking about the secular, evil, worldly meaning of the word, Lover. The word has been maligned in modern times to mean someone who uses other people for sexual exploits. We will use the word as it was meant to be, which is passionate and wholesome.

"Beloved, let us love one another: for love is of God; and every one that loveth is born of God, and knoweth God. He that loveth not knoweth not God; <u>FOR GOD IS LOVE</u>. In this was manifested the love of God toward us, because that God sent His only begotten Son into the world, that we might live through Him. Herein is Love, not that we loved God, but that He loved us, and sent His Son to be the propitiation for our sins."

1 John 4:7-10 (NASB)

As all lovers know, it is the essence and nature of LOVE to desire expression of itself. Therefore, love must have an object of its affection. And true love longs to feel this love returned, proportionate to its own expression. In other words, "Lovers long to be loved by the object of their affections, to the same extent they love them. Though true love does not require reciprocation to manifest itself, mutual adoration is desired above all things. To a Lover, unreciprocated love is the most painful and miserable of all loves. The height of joy is loving (with all our heart, mind, and soul) someone who loves us (with all their heart, mind, and soul)! This love becomes the most powerful force in the universe. It is **also** the nature of Lovers to respond to love. The greater the love is toward us, the greater the love which springs from within us. Love grows deeper and deeper throughout our lifetimes. It's no different with God, because <u>God is Love</u>. He is both an initiator of Love and <u>a responder</u> to our love.

Jesus said, "Greater love hath no man than this, that a man lay down his life for his friends."   **John 15:13 (KJV)**

Jesus demonstrated this, with His own life, toward you and me. He gave it all, to have us. How far would a man go for his bride? What would he be willing to give up to preserve her and have her forever? Everything. Jesus became a curse for us, and offered Himself up as a dying sacrifice. For a lover there is nothing so precious as the object of their affection, not even their own life.

"Christ hath redeemed (purchased) **us from the curse of the law,**(and how did He do it?) **BEING MADE** (into) **A CURSE FOR US."**   **Galatians 3:13 (KJV)**

Note Galatians 3:13 says He <u>became</u> a curse (being <u>made</u> a curse). <u>He did not become cursed. He BECAME A CURSE</u>. Remember how it was said, Ryker is human? It is a defining state of being. Here is another state of being. RYKER IS A CURSE. It is a defining state of being for all humans. Ryker is Human, therefore Ryker is a Curse. It is as simple as that. There are actually many other defining states of being as well. Ryker is a Husband, Ryker is a Father, Ryker is a Fighter, Ryker is a Lover. But, I was also a Curse. AS ADAM WAS A CURSE, SO WAS I. It is not true anymore, but it was. The reason I am not a curse anymore is because Jesus became that curse for me, and for you. As much as GOD IS LOVE, so it is just as true that JESUS WAS A CURSE.

Being a curse, what does this mean? Again, it is a state of being. Being a curse literally means everything about us, including the good, the nice, and the pleasant things about us, are so vile as to make one nauseous. It means the very best we could possibly do or ever be, always results in excrement in God's eyes. Our good intentions do not produce good, for we are evil. Therefore it is impossible for us to do righteousness. To the same extent that satan is a Curse; so were we.

Being a Curse means we cannot do anything right. It means we cannot do well at anything. It means everything coming out of our mouth also curses other people and things. It means our entire existence is completely futile, evil, and wicked. And this, no matter how nice, pleasant, loving, or generous we may be…it all comes to nothing in the end, only foundations of wood, hay and stubble consumed in fire.

"For other foundation can no man lay than that is laid, which is Jesus Christ. Now if any man build upon this foundation (Jesus) **gold, silver, precious stones, wood, hay, stubble; Every man's work shall be made manifest; for the day shall declare it, because it shall be revealed by fire; and the fire shall try every man's work of what sort it is. If any man's work abide which he hath built thereupon** (upon Jesus – the Word), **he shall receive**

a reward. **If any man's work shall be burned, he shall suffer loss: but he himself shall be saved; yet so as by fire** (because of Jesus' work)**."**

1 Corinthians 3:11-15 (KJV)

But now, if we have believed what God said about His Son, and received Jesus' sacrifice as our own, and also submit to His Lordship over our lives, we have a new state of being. *We are a Blessing*!

So, what is this state of being called a Blessing? It is the opposite of being a Curse. It means everything about us results in our Father's joy. It means we succeed at everything we set our hands to. It means everything we do, as we abide in God, makes the world a better place! Everything we do lasts forever. Everything we do produces fruit. It means our branches grow so big that the birds come by the thousands to roost in them.

"The Kingdom of Heaven (Godly spiritual dominion in *this* world beginning in our own heart**) is like a grain of mustard seed, which a man took, and sowed in his field: Which indeed is the least of all seeds: but when it is grown, it is the greatest among herbs, and becometh a tree, so that the birds of the air come and lodge in the branches thereof."** **Matthew 13:31-32 (KJV)**

Jesus' state of being has now become our state of being! He became the Curse. We became the Blessing. Now, rather than inheriting what we deserve, we inherit everything our Redeemer deserves. Everything! This is the true meaning of Grace: that we now in this life, AND in the next, receive everything Jesus deserves and has rights to.

"Truly, truly, I say to you, he who hears My word, and believes Him who sent Me, has eternal life, and does not come into judgment, but has passed out of death into life. **John 5:24 (NASB)**

I pray that the eyes of your heart may be enlightened, so that you will know what is the hope of His calling, what are the riches of the glory of His inheritance in the saints. **Ephesians 1:15 (NASB)**

This brings us to a wonderful place to ask the question then; what of His resurrection? His death certainly satisfied the bloodlust of justice. In this way, He became our Redeemer. He did not stop there, though. Three days later, He also became our Champion.

Three days later, death no longer had a sting. Three days later, there was a new sheriff in town. Hell was undone. The Law's demands (death) were met with His execution. Nevertheless, He then turned His attention to defeat death itself. He made everything new in the POWER of the resurrection…and showed us how to defeat the curse itself. Bear in mind, His single minded purpose in coming to earth, was to destroy the works of the destroyer.

"…For this purpose the Son of God was manifested, that He might DESTROY THE WORKS OF THE DEVIL." **1 John 3:8 (KJV)**

"The last enemy that shall be destroyed is <u>death</u>." **1 Cor. 15:26 (KJV)**

The curse in the Garden of Eden did far more than earn us passage to hell. It extended destruction to creation itself and to our lives here and now. It touches everything we touch in our sinful state, because we were born in unrighteousness. The decay of the world; disease, poverty, pain and depression, are the result of sin's cancerous spread.

God didn't desire for the earth to be cursed; He simply stated what was going to happen when we chose sin. After all, we were put in charge of the earth and it quite naturally reflects our spiritual condition.

In His human form, Jesus came to make all things right again; **<u>all of it!</u>** It was His desire not just to free us of the fallen condition of this world during eternity, but to free us from the effects of the curse here on earth as well. Believing anything less than this, is the worship of a lesser god. Jesus walked in righteousness on the earth, as a sinless man; and did so in the power and presence of the Holy Spirit. As a result, He had the power to do miracles; even to the extent that He was able to raise people from the dead. Through the Spirit, He also had the rightful power to be raised from the grave as well!

"But God raised Him up again, putting an end to the agony of death, since it was impossible for Him to be held in its power." **Acts 2:24 (KJV)**

"If Christ be not raised, your faith is vain; ye are yet in your sins. Then they also which are fallen asleep in Christ are perished. If in this life only we have hope in Christ, we are of all men most miserable. But now, is Christ risen from the dead and become the first fruits of them that slept. For since by man came death, by man came also the resurrection of the dead. For as in Adam all die, even so in Christ shall all be made alive."

1 Cor. 15:17-22 (KJV)

He then gave us the power to obtain this same righteousness (through the exchange of His righteousness for our unrighteousness). Because we now possess His

righteousness, though our flesh remains sinful, our spirit is already sinless through Christ Jesus! **1 John 3:9** says:

"Whosoever is born of God DOTH NOT COMMIT SIN; for His seed remaineth in him: and HE CANNOT SIN, because he is born of God. In this the children of God are manifest, and the children of the devil: WHOSOEVER DOETH NOT RIGHTEOUSNESS IS NOT OF GOD."

Because we are now righteous, we possess all His power through the same Holy Spirit who flowed through Him. With this power we establish His Kingdom upon earth by destroying the works of the destroyer and undoing the damage of the curse, IF we continue to walk in the light of Christ.

"For I know that in me (that is, in my flesh,) dwelleth no good thing: for to will is present with me; but how to perform that which is good I find not. For the good that I would I do not: but the evil which I would not, that I do. *Now if I do that I would not, it is no more I that do it, but sin that dwelleth in me.* I find then a law, that, when I would do good, evil is present with me. For I delight in the law of God after the inward man: But I see another law in my members, warring against the law of my mind, and bringing me into captivity to the law of sin which is in my members. O wretched man that I am! Who shall deliver me from the body of this death? I thank God through Jesus Christ our Lord. So then with the mind I myself serve the law of God; but with the flesh the law of sin. *There is therefore now no condemnation to them which are in Christ Jesus, "who walk not after the flesh, but after the*

Spirit. * **For the law of the Spirit of life in Christ Jesus hath made me free from the law of sin and death."**   **Romans 7:18-8:2 (KJV)**

Therefore, when He says we have the power to raise people from the dead, well then, we do!   Our Bridegroom is not only a sinless man, He is also the Almighty God. And we are His blameless Bride.

"For if, through one man, death ruled because of that man's offense, how MUCH MORE will those who receive such <u>overflowing grace and the gift of righteousness</u> RULE IN LIFE BECAUSE OF ONE MAN, JESUS CHRIST!"

Romans 5:17-18 (NASB)

Did you get that?   We can now rule and reign in THIS life, <u>IF</u> we walk in the Spirit. If we believe anything less than this, we are bowing to worship a lesser god. Jesus' victory is much more powerful than Adam's destruction.

In response to His amazing Personality, wondrous feats and awesome gifts, His Bride (you and me) reciprocates with the most precious gift we possess. We honor His immeasurable sacrifice with one of our own. We offer ourselves daily as a <u>living sacrifice</u>. Up until the moment a bride says "I Do," her choices are her own. Her future is her own (in a free society). To have her heart won by her groom changes all that though.

To say "I do," is to make the two become one. Thereafter, she no longer belongs to herself. She no longer has control of her choices, her direction, or her future. She has traded all that away in favor of becoming one with her mate. His life becomes her life, his desires become her desires, his choices become her choices, his future is now her future. Everything they do from that moment on they do together. She has become the help mete (lifegiver) to the vision of the man she chooses for herself.

It is no different when we join ourselves to Christ as His bride. There is no fifty-fifty in a godly marriage. There is only "one hundred-one hundred"! Both the Husband and Wife give their all in favor of the other. What we may have thought we wanted to do with our lives before we joined Christ is now of little relevance. Whatever His vision for our lives may be...<u>that</u> is what our lives will be. Granted, as in any godly marriage, the bride has every right, responsibility, and opportunity to be a part of the decision making process. However, the ultimate choice and responsibility for the outcome of that choice is no longer hers. A Bride ceases to live for her "self" the moment she gives her "self" away. So it is when we join ourselves unto Christ.

"I beseech you therefore, brethren, by the mercies of God, that you present your bodies a living sacrifice, holy acceptable unto God, which is your reasonable service." **Romans 12:1 (KJV)**

As in many marriages though, Christian or otherwise, not every bride is willing to give up her will, her choices, nor her future. Irregardless, the choices were made and the obligations associated with them are forever theirs. For many of us, we had no idea what we were giving up when we joined our lives to Christ. As many women do, we chose to marry with the thought in mind that marriage was all about Him taking care of us. At the very least, we married Christ merely to avoid hell. We did not sign on to actually accept any responsibility of our own. We did not sign on to submit our will, our way, or our lives. If more girls had any clue as to how much work, grief, and responsibility they were taking on before they married, few would.

Surprisingly, many girls think marriage is actually the easy way out. Joining our lives to Christ is not the easy way out either. However, for those who have joined their lives to the right mate, and have paid the price of their lives being laid down in submission…these have come to know of the magnificence of the Great Life only He can provide.

It is not the desire of our groom that we should suffer as He did. His suffering and death were meant to save us. Suffering on our part renders His suffering meaningless. His hopes are the same as mine are for my mate, that she should live abundantly and prosper. No lover gives their life in the hope that the object of their affection should suffer the same fate. How absurd is that? Jesus did what He did so we might live, and do so abundantly in every aspect of our lives. A lover does what He does in the hope of preserving and benefitting his mate. Jesus did not suffer and die needlessly. Not for me anyway. To receive anything less than what our Lover has suffered for is an indescribable and horrific waste. Make no mistake about it, if we neglect so great a salvation (not just the receiving of eternal life, but everything else He suffered for)... we will answer for it. That much is certain. Ignorance is no excuse for me, nor will it be for anyone else.

"The thief cometh not, but for to steal, and to kill, and to destroy; I AM COME THAT THEY MIGHT HAVE LIFE, AND THAT THEY MIGHT HAVE IT MORE ABUNDANTLY." **John 10:10 (KJV)**

If you have ever loved deeply, you will have no trouble understanding the measure of joy which comes to a Lover who is able to lavish upon the one they love. Lovers long to lavish all that can be had, in a daily effort, to express the depth of their affections for the one whom they adore. God's desire for us is easily demonstrated in the Garden of Eden. It is clearly evident that God's desire for Adam and Eve was that they should have Heaven upon earth. There was no curse, only blessing. The chief end of Man is revealed when God and Adam walked together in the cool of the morning.

Let's be clear though. As great as Eden was, it lacked a crucial element necessary to provide what God was attempting to create. You see, even God cannot create "true love." Not directly anyway. He can and certainly has created beings who love and even worship Him. To be truly loved by anyone though, one has to be <u>chosen</u> from amongst many other greater or equally appealing options. One must have the free choice to make. The more options a woman has, the more meaningful it is to be chosen by her.

We all enjoy the 'Beauty and the Beast' theme in love stories. You know, when the beautiful woman falls in love with the beast for what she sees inside him. When she could have had Prince Charming, she chose the Beast. We also cheer on the prince who pretends to be poor to gain the love of a woman, for who he is rather than for what he has. What was missing in the Garden of Eden? One word, "options." This was the purpose for the forbidden fruit in the garden....

As evil as the devil is, he serves a very meaningful and important purpose. His sole purpose is to do everything possible to keep us from falling in love with God. God has permitted the devil nearly every advantage, resource, and means imaginable to draw us away from God. Failing this, the devil's secondary purpose is to keep us as shallow and non-threatening as possible. There is no question, he is well armed, powerful, and highly effective at his purpose. As much pleasure as God finds in righteousness, the devil finds in being evil.

"I have created the destroyer to destroy."   **Isaiah 54:16b (KJV)**

"The thief comes <u>only</u> to steal, and kill, and destroy"   **John 10:10 (NASB)**

"And from the days of John the Baptist until now the Kingdom of Heaven suffereth violence, and the violent take it (back) *by force.***" Matt. 11:12 (KJV)**

God created us to long for Him. Blaise Pascal, a French Mathematician who lived in the 15th century wrote that he believed God created a hole in the center of our being that can ONLY be filled by Him. I believe this too. We all have this desire to be enamored by someone, and filled with something greater than ourselves. However, as a lover, God intentionally put Himself at the decided disadvantage when He created us. He literally and purposely stacked the odds against Himself.

He accomplished this in a number of ways. First of all, He created us to be "self-serving, self-centered, and self-worshipping." To make the odds more uncertain, He chose to withdraw Himself from view and reduce Himself to a small still voice. On the other hand, He permitted the devil the advantage of parading a lifetime of flashy, tempting, exciting, noisy, entertaining, enjoyable, and exhilarating, other options before us. Furthermore, while giving the devil power to give people everything they want through the flesh, He confined His ability to reach His bride to that which could only be acquired by faith.

How many lovers want to be authentically loved that bad? How many lovers do you know who would have that much confidence in the outcome they desire? How many lovers do you know who would risk losing everything, rather than accept anything less than authentic Love? How many lovers do you know who would present other lovers as being more appealing than One's Own Self? Is that crazy or what?

Every temptation in our lives is a premeditated distraction to draw us away from the Lord. While all other Lovers are showing off and doing everything possible to catch the attention and affection of those they desire, God conceals Himself. The ultimate result would undoubtedly be…. a pure unblemished Bride who has sought Him with all her heart. She will be the one who has chosen Him above all others, even over her own dreams and desires. And she will have done so against all odds to the contrary.

"By night on my bed I sought Him whom my soul loveth: I sought Him, but I found Him not. I will rise now, and go about the city in the streets, and in the broad ways. I will seek Him whom my soul loveth: I sought Him, but I found Him not. The watchmen that go about the city found me: to whom I said, 'saw ye Him whom my soul loveth?' It was but a little that I passed from them, but I found Him whom my soul loveth: I held Him, and would not let Him go." Song of Solomon 3:1-4 (KJV)

As all Lovers do, God longs to be chosen. That is the meaning of life. Don't we all want to be chosen? If it were possible to make someone love you, granted it would sure simplify things. It would most certainly eliminate all the premarital, and for some, post marital woes. Nevertheless, it would also eliminate what it feels like to be truly, truly, truly loved by someone.

Furthermore, we need to be loved not because of who we are, but despite who we are. What makes me feel most loved by my bride, is not how much she loves me for my qualities. Rather, it's how much she loves me despite my hard-to-live-with imperfections. From the very beginning, we were two of the most incompatible people as one may ever find. How then have we succeeded in love for one another? Not because it was easy. Quite the contrary, it was brutal.

The trouble is that there is a God-given reason opposites attract. People in today's society generally move from one relationship to the next, seeking a compatible mate. When they discover this new one is incompatible, they separate or divorce, and move onto the next relationship. What they are actually looking for is someone who will require the least amount of change from them as possible. It is chalked up to irreconcilable differences. They want the benefits associated with a covenant marriage, just without the price. The next best thing is a contract marriage. "I am going to love you forever or until you stop making me happy, whichever comes first." This is quite different from the covenant marriage which simply says, "I am going to Love you forever, no matter how much it may cost me."

Contract marriage folks don't realize that in their self-serving choice, they have already missed the best part of love. True love, is therefore absolutely unobtainable. Contract marriages are nothing more than a weak, self-serving, cheap imitation of the real thing. True Love is meant to be hard, it's meant to change us, it's meant to cost us something (usually everything). True love demonstrates that the object of our affection is more precious than even our own deepest desires. True love demonstrates that the object of our affection, is our deepest desire. You see, compatible love is only about pleasing "number one." Incompatible love on the other hand, is about loving someone else more than ourselves.

Compatible people <u>CANNOT</u> know the depth of love which <u>ONLY</u> exists between incompatible people. That is, incompatible people who have loved each other through the harshest of circumstances, and changed completely for the benefit of one another. They are the happiest of all people, and the only ones who enjoy true love. Don't get me wrong, I am not suggesting that people intentionally marry an incompatible mate. You see, unless both mates are willing to change, marrying an incompatible mate is a recipe for disaster.

So there you have it. The secret to true love is that it is only obtainable to people who are willing to change. Only in this way, do I and my mate know how much we love each other. We are known by how much we have willingly MADE ourselves compatible. The idea of "being willing" to give our life for our mate, and "actually doing it" every day are two entirely different things. God desires this level of intimacy with us, and He longs for it with you. He is a Lover. Trust me, you are all He can think about.

He desires for you, what I desire for my own wife: all the good in this life that can be given her. To be her provider, protector, lover, leader, and her best friend; these are my chief goals. There exists no doubt, in her mind, how I respond to threats against her. She has seen my love for her. She has seen that it is her fierce protector. She has seen that it does not merely stand against big threats. It also stands against the small ones, the ones that may merely deprive her of a smile. Anything that does not make her smile, contradicts every ounce of love I have for her. When she hurts, it's personal. That is unavoidable. Nothing she feels is isolated to her. All of it, I feel.

So it is with God, in regard to His bride. God is Love. Everything I know about being a husband, I learned from Him loving me. The point in all this discussion should be clear by now. Godly marriage between a man and a woman is our God-given visual representation of what He longs for with us. The godly institution of marriage teaches us everything we need to know about how God feels about us, relates to us, and thinks about us. That is its primary purpose.

The vast majority of people misunderstand the love of God entirely. If they correctly conceive in their minds that God's love is unconditional, most mistakenly conclude that His blessings must be as well. Jesus does say that the rain (life giving water) falls on the just and unjust, because God loves all people, and the world must continue on its course. But to take all Scripture into account, we must be aware that there are special blessings stored up for those that live their lives under His refuge. Most people believe that since God is Love, He should bless even those who have no affection for Him at all. So most go about living their lives as autonomous souls, doing whatever they please. Then when suffering advances, these same people get angry with God when He does not give them what they pray for.

Almost all people are really asking for a genie in a bottle, not a personal God. While most Christians buy into the "bumper sticker ideology" that says God is a personal God, they have no intention of actually being His friend, much less His mate. So it amazes me when Christians play the harlot with other gods, then blame God when things go south on them. Relationships and true love are difficult. They can't be had without changing and serving each other. Relationships have to be nurtured every day, in order to be available for us at the times we need them the most. If a person only lives for themselves, in the end all they will have is themselves.

Loving my wife has always meant denying what I felt like I deserved. It always meant doing the hard things when there were easier more appealing options. It meant eating a lot of crow. It meant lots of heart break, humiliation, and hurt feelings. Mostly, it meant being a man and sucking it up. The reason for choosing to be a man was that the reward (a relationship with her) was so important to me. Any pain associated with the process was always infinitely worth the price paid.

In the same way, there is a reason I have a relationship with the Lord that results in this level of intimacy. I have nurtured it, as I nurture the one with my wife. Loving Him more than myself always meant doing the hard things. It meant making the difficult choices. It meant giving up what I thought I deserved, and not going the way I wanted to go. It meant surrender. But, I wanted the reward (a relationship with Him) so bad that any pain associated with the process was infinitely worth the price paid.

People who listen, often hear me say "Dig your well before you get thirsty." Almost all people want what God has to offer, this much is true. However, they only want it when they have lost complete control and something really bad has happened. Then they are angry with Him when He does not jump in and fix it immediately. Often, they may even attempt to bargain with Him, about increasing their devotion if He will help them. Truthfully though, they have no intention of doing anything other than going back to their autonomous relationship of ignoring Him; once normalcy is reacquired.

How many divorced men do we all know who hate women because their ex-wives (multiple) got tired of being ignored, unappreciated, and unloved? These men reason that they are a magnet for lousy women. It never crosses their mind, that possibly their ex-wives were merely magnets for a lousy husband. Do you want a wife who will love you when you are old and frail? Try loving her more than yourself for the rest of your life. You want God to be there for you when you need Him the most? Try loving Him more than you love yourself for the rest of your life.

"ALL WE like sheep, have gone astray, WE HAVE EVERYONE TURNED TO HIS OWN WAY; and the Lord hath laid Him the iniquity of us all." Is. 53:6 (KJV)

The truth is, we have ALL played the harlot. We all have had many husbands, and the one we live with now is not even our husband. (John 4:7-19). It is fact; nobody can experience the true love of another unless they are their ONLY love. True love not only desires to be the only love, it desires to be the only love **EVER**. To give any part of one's self away, which rightfully belongs to our mate (even before they are our mate), robs their mate of something they can never get back. It is a bitter betrayal. Before marriage it's called "Fornication." After marriage, it's called "Adultery." These are different words that really mean the same thing. Giving something away to another that belongs to our mate, not to us. We have sold what is precious to our mate, at yard sale prices. We have played the harlot with our Groom, the Lord Jesus Christ.

"Now concerning the things whereof ye wrote unto me: It is good for a man not to touch a woman. Nevertheless, to avoid fornication, let every man have his own wife, and let every woman have her own husband. Let the husband render unto the wife due benevolence: and likewise also the wife unto the husband. THE WIFE HATH NOT POWER OF HER OWN BODY, BUT THE HUSBAND. AND LIKEWISE ALSO THE HUSBAND HATH NOT POWER OF HIS OWN BODY, BUT THE WIFE."   1 Corinthians 7:1-4 (KJV)

"For thou SHALT WORSHIP NO OTHER GOD (including your "Self"): **for the Lord, WHOSE NAME IS JEALOUS, is a jealous God."   Exodus 34:14 (KJV)**

This being said, the ultimate relationship is the one between two people who are doing everything possible to out-love the other. In this marriage, there are no limits to the desire one has for the other; except as human limitations may dictate. While we might like to lasso the moon for our bride, it's just not really possible. For God though, it is!

So, let's get back to the subject of ABANDONED BLESSINGS.

Understanding what abandoned blessings are, begins with understanding how much God longs to bless us. Furthermore, we must then have a thorough understanding of what those blessings are. With no knowledge of them, they are simply not available. There is only one way to know what they are. We must know His Word. And we must know that there is only one way to get those blessings: by Faith. What are abandoned blessings? They are unaccessed and untapped blessings that have always been available to us, as His people. They are the benefits that come with being engaged to the King of kings, and will meet the needs for every aspect of our life.

Let's be clear. No matter how long we may live, we shall never be able to measure the breadth of God's blessings prepared and available for us. However, the little that can be grasped defies the wildest imagination. There are thousands of promises to be found, in the Scriptures, and having done so we would still only be scratching at the surface. Here are a few to consider:

DEUTERONOMY 28:1-13 SAYS YOU WILL BE BLESSED:

1. IN THE CITY	10. YOUR STOREHOUSES
2. IN THE FIELD	11. ALL YOUR WORK
3. YOUR CHILDREN	12. YOUR HOME
4. YOUR LAND	13. PLENTIFUL GOODS
5. YOUR INCOME	14. PLENTY OF CHILDREN
6. YOUR FOOD	15. PLENTY OF INCOME
7. WHEN YOU COME IN	16. ALL YOUR LABORS
8. WHEN YOU GO OUT	17. LEND, NEVER BORROW
9. ENEMIES DESTROYED	18. THE HEAD; NOT TAIL.
	19. ABOVE, NOT BENEATH

"And ye shall serve the Lord your God, and HE SHALL BLESS THY BREAD, and THY WATER; and I WILL TAKE SICKNESS AWAY from the midst of thee."

Exodus 23:25 (KJV)

"You shall SPEND your DAYS in PROSPERITY and your YEARS in PLEASURE.

Job 36:11 (KJV)

"My kindness will NEVER depart from you. NEITHER will my COVENANT OF PEACE with you ever be REMOVED....I will lay your stones with fair colors, and lay your foundations with sapphires. And I will make your windows of agate, and your gates of carbuncles, and all your borders with pleasant stones. All your children will be taught by the Lord; and GREAT will be your children's PEACE. In RIGHTEOUSNESS you will be ESTABLISHED; you will be FAR FROM OPPRESSION; BECAUSE you will NOT FEAR ANYTHING, and from terror, because IT WILL NOT COME NEAR YOU...NO WEAPON FORMED AGAINST YOU WILL EVER HURT YOU."   Isaiah 54:10-17 (paraphrase)

"You will CAST OUT DEVILS, you will SPEAK WITH UNKNOWN LANGUAGES, you will TAKE UP SERPENTS and other DEADLY things and THEY WON'T BE ABLE TO HURT YOU. If you DRINK any DEADLY thing, it WILL NOT HURT YOU. When you LAY HANDS on the SICK, they WILL RECOVER."

Mark 16:17-18 (paraphrase)

"Behold, I give unto you POWER to TRED on SERPENTS, SCORPIONS, and ANYTHING ELSE, that normally hurts and kills other people. And YOU will be GIVEN AUTHORITY OVER ALL the POWER of the DEVIL, and NOTHING BY ANY MEANS POSSIBLE WILL BE ABLE TO HURT YOU."   Luke 10:19 (paraphrase)

"Truly, Truly, I say to you, he who believes in Me, the works that I do shall he do also; and GREATER WORKS THAN THESE SHALL HE DO; because I go to the Father."   John 14:12-13 NASB

"...I will open you the WINDOWS OF HEAVEN, and POUR YOU OUT A BLESSING, that there SHALL NOT BE ROOM ENOUGH TO RECEIVE IT." Malachi 3:10 (KJV)

"But thou shalt remember the Lord thy God: for it is He that GIVETH THEE POWER TO GET WEALTH, that He may ESTABLISH His COVENANT which He SWARE unto thy fathers, AS IT IS THIS DAY."   Deuteronomy 8:18 (KJV)

"You will receive a HUNDRED TIMES back WHATEVER you invest in the Kingdom of Heaven, while living on this earth, as well as in eternity."

Mark 10:29 (paraphrase)

"You will have a LONG LIFE."   Deut. 30:19-20 (paraphrase)

PSALMS 91 PROMISES:

1. **Divine protection of the Almighty God**
2. **He is your Refuge and Fortress.**
3. **Deliverance from traps.**
4. **Deliverance from belligerent disease.**
5. **Divine covering from all threats.**
6. **Protection from threats that sneak into our lives under the cover of darkness, as well as those that come at us in broad daylight.**
7. **Absolute protection from unknown and unexpected disease, as well as disease that we recognize is affecting everyone else out in the open.**
8. **Confidence that, no matter what happens to other people around us, the bad stuff hurting them cannot come near us.**
9. **Confidence that we will only observe the evil that happens to others.**
10. **No evil will fall upon you, nor come near anything that is yours.**
11. **You can walk on things that hurt other people, and it will not be able to hurt you.**

12. **He Loves you, He will deliver you, He will exalt you.**
13. **When we call out to Him, He will always answer.**
14. **He will deliver you and He will honor you.**
15. **He will satisfy you with a long life and then show you Heaven.**

Even as we scratch the surface of the enormous blessings intended for us, we are immediately compelled to ask a staggering question. If these blessings are ours, then "How is it possible that so many Christians would deprive themselves of them?" It is startling to realize how much we leave behind and deny ourselves, through ignorance and unbelief. It stands to reason, had these blessings been as apparent to me then as they are now; I could have easily found my own way to the "Secret Place." Without this revelation, ignorance would have withheld them from me forever.

Years ago, the Lord spoke to me out of Isaiah 58:12. There, He spoke of rebuilding the ancient ruins and the desolation of many generations. In context, He is referring to the rebuilding of Jerusalem. However this passage also speaks well, as a metaphor, about the rebuilding of the Kingdom of Heaven which the city of Jerusalem (Zion) itself represents.

This understanding has been lost for nearly two thousand years. Somewhere, soon after the latter end of the book of Acts, the truth of human authority was lost, and people focused only on one aspect of Jesus' work: that of salvation from sin only. All the other benefits Jesus paid the price to win back from the enemy's clutches were long forgotten. Christ's work was reduced to an evangelistic fire insurance plan, an inheritance we obtain only after WE die.

He laboriously attempted to help His disciples understand that the redemption of creation itself was to be an exciting partnership between Him and His Bride. He patiently taught them how to push the enemy back into the far corners of the earth, essentially making the destroyer inconsequential and impotent. Unfortunately, these concepts were bigger than their ability to pass to the next generation. The trials which came upon the church at that time were gigantic. Standing in faith as a spiritual conqueror, therefore became lost in a suffering ideology. The responsibility for rebuilding the ancient ruins passed unperceived and unreceived from one generation to the next. Now, it has fallen upon the shoulders of this generation.

"The highest heavens belong to the Lord, BUT THE EARTH HE HAS GIVEN TO MAN."   **Psalm 115:16-17 (NIV)**

"When I consider Thy heavens, the work of Thy fingers, the moon and the stars, which Thou hast ordained; WHAT IS MAN, THAT THOU ART MINDFUL OF HIM? and THE SON OF MAN, THAT THOU VISITEST HIM? For Thou hast made him a little lower than the angels, and HAST CROWNED HIM WITH GLORY AND HONOUR. THOU HAST MADEST HIM TO HAVE DOMINION OVER THE WORKS OF THY HANDS; THOU HAST PUT ALL THINGS UNDER HIS FEET."

                                                            Psalm 8:3-6 (KJV)

While Jesus' blood, shed for us, remains central to Christian teaching, the broken body of Christ has long been forsaken under mountains of pain, disappointment, and unbelief. We remember why His blood was shed, but we have forgotten why His body was broken. We no longer believe His promises. Instead, we build our doctrines upon what happens to people; rather than what God's Word actually says. We find it easier to believe God wants to hurt us than to bless us. Expecting nothing always guarantees we won't be disappointed. Expecting great things though? That takes a great deal of faith and the effort associated with it. It will always be easier to plan for the worst than to expect the best.

Nevertheless, it still amazes me that we would incarcerate a father who abuses his children, while on the other hand, choose to worship a god who maims and kills his children, supposedly for the "better good." Brothers and sisters this ought not be so. It is never acceptable for a father to injure, maim, or kill His children, even for a good reason. <u>Especially if He is God</u>. To think that there is ever a good reason to do evil to one's children, especially for God, is absolutely ludicrous.

Because of this ignorance and unbelief, many healings remain untouched. They are stored away for as long as we remain in unbelief. The sad possibility is that almost all Christians may arrive in Heaven, only to find warehouses full of blessings intended for them while on earth. As for me, my chief aim when that day comes, is that there will be nothing but a few empty cardboard boxes lying about and a shipping label or two drifting in with the wind. My heart despises the thought that anything of my earthly inheritance should remain untouched. And so, as my wife does me, I always turn my face toward my Husband. Far above all things of this earth, I seek Him with all my heart and favor Him; especially over my "self." For that reason, it pleases me to receive His affections.

"If ye then, being evil (compared to God), **know how to give good gifts unto your children, how MUCH MORE shall your Father which is in Heaven give good things to them that ask Him?"** Matthew 7:11 (KJV)

The Enclaves

What do these Enclaves represent and what is their significance? They certainly are one of the most central features throughout all the visions. They are one of the only things that never change. In the visions, it never occurred to me to question Him on details like this. It was natural to just readily accept whatever He said. If He wanted to call them enclaves or envelopes, it made no difference to me. Since He is God and I am not, letting Him define anything the way He liked always seemed the prudent thing to do. Interestingly though, here is a generally accepted English language definition of the word "Enclave." You are free to consider it in any manner you like. According to the dictionary, an enclave is: "a country, kingdom, or territory almost entirely surrounded by the country, kingdom, or territory of another."

What does this mean, and how does it relate to this secret place?

The church building itself represents me and my life. It may just as easily represent you and your life as well, if you find it relevant as such. It may also be said to quite accurately represent the present day church body at large. Inside the chapel (that is inside me), we find these enclaves (Him) which represent His Territory. The Enclaves are His. However, what is inside them is mine once He opens the door and gives the contents to me. These enclaves appear to be places where He has stored everything necessary for life and godliness. To obtain these things, it has been necessary to ask for them. He always knows which one contains what is needed. He leads the way to it, and presents its contents to me. So, it's easy to look at it this way: Contained within me, we find these enclaves of His kingdom. In this same way God has an enclave in all of our hearts, in all of our lives, through His Holy Spirit. That is, in those of us who know Him and walk with Him.

For those savvy in the Scriptures, there will be an immediately recognizable event these thoughts bring to mind. Recall, if you will, what Jesus had to say to the Samaritan woman at the well. He spoke to her of a special kind of water. He called it living water. If she drank this water, she would never thirst again. She thought this kind of water was just what she needed, so she would not have to keep coming to the well.

Though she did not comprehend the nature of the water He spoke of, at the moment, she was nevertheless not far off. In reality, He was telling her that she herself would

become the well from which the Holy Spirit would flow through. Living water would spring up from within her. In this way, she would never lack for spiritual water (life) again. She would have to go no further to find living water than there within her, in the person of the Holy Spirit.

He went on to explain that she would no longer need go to the mountain to worship Him either. The mountain would be within her. We also learn from lessons following this one, that she would no longer be restricted from the Holy of Holies. For the Holy of Holies would be within her. So it is, for each of us, the very instant we receive Christ as our Savior. Our very first enclaves are set up the moment we utter the repentant words of our heart toward Him.

The things we need most are given to us. Things like forgiveness, redemption, and salvation. In surrendering to His Lordship over the course of our lives, as we mature, we have new enclaves made available to us. Each of them collectively provide <u>everything</u> necessary for our lives, and for becoming like Him (godliness). In the moment we need them, they are there ready for us.

The significance of the numerous enclaves was not understandable to me, until only very recently. It was much easier to visualize the concept of a warehouse. What of these small individual armoires though? And, why did each of them contain something different?

Here is how it appears to manifest itself in real life. Life simply does not work like it does in the warehouse metaphor. "How is that?" you say. The warehouse concept implies that once a person works out the details of faith, they can just walk in and get everything they need. It leaves one with the impression that walking in faith is a one-time event. But faith is not a single event.

Each and every blessing or miracle comes with a reflection upon past successes, true enough. Nevertheless, each one still requires new faith to rise up from within us to meet the need of the moment. Faith is something one has to actively choose daily. Furthermore, it will be pitted against insurmountable temptations to not believe. We are always going to have CHOOSE to walk by faith and not by sight. When everything says we are not healed this time, we must rise up against that evil report and declare our own righteous report which agrees with His Word. You have already been given a few Scriptures which reveal His will regarding healing:

Ex.23:25, Mark 16:17-18, Luke 10:19 and Psalm 91:3,6 and 10 to name just a few. Trust me though and search them out, there are many more.

We must <u>NEVER EVER</u> utter with our lips satan's lie, "Well, it might be God's will for me not to be healed." The same Christian who can utter such foolish things about their god will have no trouble uttering that about their own children. Imagine yourself saying:"Sweetheart, it's just not my will for you to be healed from this sickness, you can learn so much from it. That is why I can't give you this medicine the Doctor prescribed."

If you can say that about your children, then really do us all a favor and turn yourself into the authorities. If you would never dream of sayings such a crazy thing, then please do me a favor and quit accusing my God of saying it to you. Are you so much better a father or mother than He? If so, you seriously need a new god. Just because our manifested answer may take time, does not mean it is not ours or that it has been denied us. If we walk by faith, then the result of Him supplying more faith will be our reward. If we walk by sight, then the result of our own natural (limited) sight will be our reward. Either way, the result is a matter of our capacity to believe, not whether He is fit to be a Father.

So it has been every time I go to my secret place, and take something away. I have to believe all over again. I do have to be honest here, I have not succeeded every time in believing and receiving everything He has given me. As a result, some of the healings and answers I got would inevitably be stolen from me. A few came back. (Matthew 13:1-23) However, each time my Lord would ultimately take them back from my adversary; and again return them to me. That is, if I chose to repent of my unbelief, turn again to His face, asking and believing.

"As it is written, 'I have made thee (Abraham) **a father of many nations, before Him whom he believed, even God, who quickeneth the dead, and CALLETH THOSE THINGS WHICH BE NOT AS THOUGH THEY** (already) **WERE. Who against hope believed in hope, that he might become the father of many nations; according to that which was spoken, So shall thy seed be. AND BEING NOT WEAK IN FAITH, HE CONSIDERED NOT HIS OWN BODY now dead, when he was about an hundred years old, neither yet the deadness of Sarah's womb: He STAGGERED NOT AT THE PROMISE OF GOD THROUGH UNBELIEF; BUT WAS STRONG IN FAITH, GIVING GLORY TO GOD. AND BEING FULLY PERSUADED THAT, WHAT HE HAD PROMISED, HE WAS ABLE ALSO TO PERFORM.' And therefore it was imputed to him for righteousness. NOW IT WAS NOT WRITTEN FOR HIS SAKE ALONE, that it was imputed to him; BUT FOR US ALSO, to whom it shall be imputed, if we believe on Him that raised up Jesus our Lord from the dead."** Romans 4:17-24 (KJV)

Permission to Heal

It may come as a surprise to those who never considered this. God does not heal anyone against their will. The Holy Spirit is a gentleman. He does not force anything on anyone's body. In every case, God always asks for permission to do so. Here in my secret place, you will always see Him asking or offering. Naturally, the idea that a person would reject healing seems absurd. But let's not be naive. People, for the most part, are absurd. Three essential elements come to mind, that determine whether healing will be received or not: Free-will, authority, and faith.

Regarding Free-Will: Come sink or swim, come heck or high water, come life or death, we are free to choose our own paths. It's as simple as that. And, even if it kills us, God will not violate nor deny us our right to choose. One of the most troubling things about living in America is all our freedoms. "How is that troubling?" you ask. In order to have the freedoms we have, we are compelled to allow everyone, even people we don't like, to have theirs as well. Many of these people have horrible ideas. To have our freedom to choose, though, we have to equally protect everyone else's freedom to choose. You see, it's a slippery slope when we begin to govern the thoughts and choices of others. It may seem great to govern other's thoughts when we are in the position of being able to do so. However, when the tables turn (and they will), then it will be they who are governing our thoughts.

In the same way, God respects everyone's right to choose. He guards this right, even to the detriment, and often times even unto the death of ourselves and others. Our right to life, liberty, and the pursuit of happiness, is absolute. In America, we believe God gave us our rights. However, these freedoms can often get out of hand. By human nature, we are all self-absorbed. So the laws in our country give us freedom, but with stipulations. Our rights of choice are absolute only up to the point where they begin to deny other's their equally justified rights of choice.

To insure that these freedoms are equally enjoyed by all, we have the judicial branch of government. The judicial branch of government enforces the laws that govern our rights. This branch has the authority to deny individuals their rights, when those individuals have interfered in the rights of others. For example, one's pursuit of happiness may involve taking things that don't belong to them. In the act of that pursuit, the individual has interfered in the right of another to enjoy what he has rightfully earned – or his pursuit of happiness. A judge therefore has the right to deny the transgressor his rights by imprisoning him. And in the case of one whom has taken the life of another, they may even be required to forfeit their own life in repayment.

By this token, we each have the freedom to choose our own path. As a human created in the image of God, each man has the free will to choose the ideologies which will govern his or her life, so long as in doing so, they do not deprive another of the equal enjoyment of theirs. If a person chooses to worship a god that hurts and does not heal, then it is their god-given right to do so. And even God Himself will not deprive that person of their free-choice. We can reach out to that person and offer, but we are not at liberty to force upon a person freedom from their bondage. While you may be able to lead a horse to water, you cannot make them drink.

Regarding authority: Law enforcement personnel obtain their authority; they are not born with it. They are elected, or appointed by people whom have the authority to do so. In America, that authority is derived from the people. Ultimately, all authority that exists is derived from God. He is the center of all power in the universe. And, we learn from Scripture that He delegated His authority over this world to mankind. This began with Adam.

"The heavens are the LORD'S: but the earth hath He given to the children of men." **Psalm 115:16-17 (KJV)**

"And God said, Let us make man in our image, after our likeness: and let them have dominion over the fish of the sea, and over the fowl ofthe air, and over the cattle, and over all the earth, and over every creeping thing that creepeth upon the earth." **Genesis 1:26 (KJV)**

"When I consider Thy heavens, the work of Thy fingers, the moon and the stars, which Thou hast ordained; WHAT IS MAN, THAT THOU ART MINDFUL OF HIM? and THE SON OF MAN, THAT THOU VISITEST HIM? For Thou hast made him a little lower than the angels, and HAST CROWNED HIM WITH GLORY AND HONOUR. <u>THOU HAST MADEST HIM TO HAVE DOMINION OVER THE WORKS OF THY HANDS; THOU HAST PUT ALL THINGS UNDER HIS FEET."</u> **Psalm 8:3-6**

When Adam rebelled against God, He was not cast from earth. He was cast from the Garden where God was. What is the significance of this? It's clear from Psalm 8, that mankind never lost their authority over the earth. But, he was cut off from the center of power (God) that gave him his authority. He was placed under a curse and denied access to the life intended for him. Now, when Adam tried to keep bad things from happening in his life; he was like a police officer without a gun, barking orders at a killer who is armed with an assault rifle. Authority without the power to back it up is nothing more than a toothless lion.

As a result, it has been pretty darn difficult for Adam's descendants to get any respect from the destroyer. And it does not take a toothless lion long to start feeling like a toothless lion, so we gave up trying. Average human beings have resorted to a lethargic state, not knowing what to do when the enemy comes into their lives stealing, killing, and destroying. Most of the time, satan doesn't even glance in their direction as he takes them out, much less display any fear of these creatures created in God's image. All the power satan possesses on this earth was given him by default, in the absence of those who would have taken back the Kingdom by force.

"All that is necessary for evil to triumph, is for good (God's) people to do nothing."   -Edmund Burke

The Garden of Eden manifested the blessed life of a relationship right with God. It was the "Kingdom of Heaven" upon this earth. It was where God's will was done upon earth, "as it was in Heaven." However Adam (and us with him) became accursed and were pushed outside this Kingdom of Heaven. So, now we all find ourselves standing on the outside of blessings; where there is weeping and gnashing our teeth. As we look inside, all we can do is wish for what can no longer be ours upon this earth. That is, if it were not for the completed work of Christ. God had a plan for our salvation. Jesus appeared upon the earth to <u>become the curse for us, to shed His blood for our soul, and to have His body broken for our body</u>. In this way, all things have been made new. Only in this can the power of His last words, "It is finished," be truly appreciated.

Our Lord has plundered the enemy's camp, and taken back all that was rightfully ours to begin with! Satan, who usurped his position from the rightful heirs NEVER had authority to do so. Now, he no longer has any power over us either. We have the authority, and access to the power center of God's Holy Spirit has been restored to us as well, if we have been born again.

"Christ hath redeemed us from the curse of the law, BEING MADE A CURSE FOR US; for it is written, cursed is everyone that hangeth on a tree (the cross)**: THAT THE BLESSING OF ABRAHAM MIGHT COME ON THE GENTILES through Jesus Christ..."**   **Galatians 3:13-14 (KJV)**

What is the curse He is talking about?

Deuteronomy 28: 15-68

"...It shall come to pass, IF THOU WILT NOT HEARKEN UNTO THE VOICE OF THE LORD THY GOD, to observe to do all his commandments and His statutes which I command thee this day; that ALL THESE CURSES SHALL COME UPON THEE, AND OVERTAKE THEE.

<u>Cursed shalt thou be in the city</u>, and <u>cursed shalt thou be in the field</u>.

<u>Cursed shall be thy basket and thy store.</u>

<u>Cursed shall be the fruit of thy body, and the fruit of thy land, the increase of thy kine, and the flocks of thy sheep.</u>

<u>Cursed shalt thou be when thou comest in, and cursed shalt thou be when thou goest out.</u>

<u>The LORD shall send upon thee</u> cursing, vexation, and rebuke, in all that thou settest thine hand unto for to do, until thou be destroyed, and until thou perish quickly; because of the wickedness of thy doings, whereby thou hast forsaken me.

<u>The LORD shall make</u> the pestilence cleave unto thee, until he have consumed thee from off the land, whither thou goest to possess it.

<u>The LORD shall smite</u> thee with consumption, and with a fever, and with an inflammation, and with an extreme burning, and with the sword, and with blasting, and with mildew; and they shall pursue thee until thou perish.

And thy Heaven that is over thy head shall be brass (impenetrable), and the earth that is under thee shall be iron.

<u>The LORD shall make</u> the rain of thy land powder and dust: from Heaven shall it come down upon thee, until thou be destroyed.

<u>The LORD shall cause</u> thee to be smitten before thine enemies: thou shalt go out one way against them, and flee seven ways before them: and shalt be removed into all the kingdoms of the earth. And thy carcass shall be meat unto all fowls of the air, and unto the beasts of the earth, and no man shall fray them away.

The LORD will smite thee with the botch of Egypt, and with the emerods, and with the scab, and with the itch, whereof thou canst not be healed.

The LORD shall smite thee with madness, and blindness, and astonishment of heart:

And thou shalt grope at noonday, as the blind gropeth in darkness, and thou shalt not prosper in thy ways: and thou shalt be only oppressed and spoiled evermore, and no man shall save thee.

Thou shalt betroth a wife, and another man shall lie with her: thou shalt build an house, and thou shalt not dwell therein: thou shalt plant a vineyard, and shalt not gather the grapes thereof.

Thine ox shall be slain before thine eyes, and thou shalt not eat thereof: thine ass shall be violently taken away from before thy face, and shall not be restored to thee: thy sheep shall be given unto thine enemies, and thou shalt have none to rescue them.

Thy sons and thy daughters shall be given unto another people, and thine eyes shall look, and fail with longing for them all the day long; and there shall be no might in thine hand.

The fruit of thy land, and all thy labours, shall a nation which thou knowest not eat up; and thou shalt be only oppressed and crushed alway:

So that thou shalt be mad for the sight of thine eyes which thou shalt see.

The LORD shall smite thee in the knees, and in the legs, with a sore botch that cannot be healed, from the sole of thy foot unto the top of thy head.

The LORD shall bring thee, and thy king which thou shalt set over thee, unto a nation which neither thou nor thy fathers have known; and there shalt thou serve other gods, wood and stone.

And thou shalt become astonishment, a proverb, and a byword, among all nations whither the LORD shall lead thee.

Thou shalt carry much seed out into the field, and shalt gather but little in; for the locust shall consume it.

Thou shalt plant vineyards, and dress them, but shalt neither drink of the wine, nor gather the grapes; for the worms shall eat them.

Thou shalt have olive trees throughout all thy coasts, but thou shalt not anoint thyself with the oil; for thine olive shall cast his fruit.

Thou shalt beget sons and daughters, but thou shalt not enjoy them; for they shall go into captivity.

All thy trees and fruit of thy land shall the locust consume.

The stranger that is within thee shall get up above thee very high; and thou shalt come down very low.

He shall lend to thee, and thou shalt not lend to him: he shall be the head, and thou shalt be the tail.

<u>Moreover all these curses shall come upon thee, and shall pursue thee, and overtake thee, till thou be destroyed; because thou hearkenedst not unto the voice of the LORD thy God, to keep his commandments and his statutes which he commanded thee</u>:

<u>And they shall be upon thee for a sign and for a wonder, and upon thy seed forever</u>.

Because thou servedst not the LORD thy God with joyfulness, and with gladness of heart, for the abundance of all things;

Therefore shalt thou serve thine enemies which the LORD shall send against thee, in hunger, and in thirst, and in nakedness, and in want of all things: and he shall put a yoke of iron upon thy neck, until he have destroyed thee.

The LORD shall bring a nation against thee from far, from the end of the earth, as swift as the eagle flieth; a nation whose tongue thou shalt not understand; A nation of fierce countenance, which shall not regard the person of the old, nor shew favour to the young: And he shall eat the fruit of thy cattle, and the fruit of thy land, until thou be destroyed: which also shall not leave thee either corn, wine, or oil, or the increase of thy kine, or flocks of thy sheep, until he have destroyed thee.

And he shall besiege thee in all thy gates, until thy high and fenced walls come down, wherein thou trustedst, throughout all thy land: and he shall besiege thee in all thy gates throughout all thy land, which the LORD thy God hath given thee.

And thou shalt eat the fruit of thine own body, the flesh of thy sons and of thy daughters, which the LORD thy God hath given thee, in the siege, and in the straitness, wherewith thine enemies shall distress thee:

So that the man that is tender among you, and very delicate, his eye shall be evil toward his brother, and toward the wife of his bosom, and toward the remnant of his children which he shall leave:

So that he will not give to any of them of the flesh of his children whom he shall eat: because he hath nothing left him in the siege, and in the straitness, wherewith thine enemies shall distress thee in all thy gates.

The tender and delicate woman among you, which would not adventure to set the sole of her foot upon the ground for delicateness and tenderness, her eye shall be evil toward the husband of her bosom, and toward her son, and toward her daughter,

And toward her young one that cometh out from between her feet, and toward her children which she shall bear: for she shall eat them for want of all things secretly in the siege and straitness, wherewith thine enemy shall distress thee in thy gates.

If thou wilt not observe to do all the words of this law that are written in this book, that thou mayest fear this glorious and fearful name, THE LORD THY GOD; Then the LORD will make thy plagues wonderful, and the plagues of thy seed, even great plagues, and of long continuance, and sore sicknesses, and of long continuance.

Moreover He will bring upon thee all the diseases of Egypt, which thou wast afraid of; and they shall cleave unto thee.Also every sickness, and every plague, which is not written in the book of this law, them will the LORD bring upon thee, until thou be destroyed.

And ye shall be left few in number, whereas ye were as the stars of Heaven for multitude; because thou wouldest not obey the voice of the LORD thy God.

And it shall come to pass, that as the LORD rejoiced over you to do you good, and to multiply you; so the LORD will rejoice over you to destroy you, and to bring you to nought; and ye shall be plucked from off the land whither thou goest to possess it.

And the LORD shall scatter thee among all people, from the one end of the earth even unto the other; and there thou shalt serve other gods, which neither thou nor thy fathers have known, even wood and stone.

And among these nations shalt thou find no ease, neither shall the sole of thy foot have rest: but the LORD shall give thee there a trembling heart, and failing of eyes, and sorrow of mind:

And thy life shall hang in doubt before thee; and thou shalt fear day and night, and shalt have none assurance of thy life:

In the morning thou shalt say, Would God it were even! and at even thou shalt say, Would God it were morning! for the fear of thine heart wherewith thou shalt fear, and for the sight of thine eyes which thou shalt see.

And the LORD shall bring thee into Egypt again with ships, by the way whereof I spake unto thee, Thou shalt see it no more again: and there ye shall be sold unto your enemies for bondmen and bondwomen, and no man shall buy you." (KJV)

And what is the Blessing of Abraham that has come upon us because of The Completed Work of Christ?

Deuteronomy 28:1-14

"...It shall come to pass, **IF THOU SHALT DILIGENTLY HEARKEN** unto the voice of the LORD thy God, to observe and to do all his commandments which I command thee this day, that the LORD thy God will set thee on high above all nations of the earth:

And <u>ALL THESE BLESSINGS SHALL COME ON THEE, AND OVERTAKE THEE, if thou shalt hearken unto the voice of the LORD thy God.</u>

<u>Blessed shalt thou be in the city, and blessed shalt thou be in the field.</u>

Blessed shall be the fruit of thy body, and the fruit of thy ground, and the fruit of thy cattle, the increase of thy kine, and the flocks of thy sheep.

Blessed shall be thy basket and thy store.

Blessed shalt thou be when thou comest in, and blessed shalt thou be when thou goest out.

The LORD shall cause thine enemies that rise up against thee to be smitten before thy face: they shall come out against thee one way, and flee before thee seven ways.

The LORD shall command the blessing upon thee in thy storehouses, and in all that thou settest thine hand unto; and He shall bless thee in the land which the LORD thy God giveth thee.

The LORD shall establish thee an holy people unto Himself, as He hath sworn unto thee, if thou shalt keep the commandments of the LORD thy God, and walk in His ways. And all people of the earth shall see that thou art called by the name of the LORD; and they shall be afraid of thee.

And the LORD shall make thee plenteous in goods, in the fruit of thy body, and in the fruit of thy cattle, and in the fruit of thy ground, in the land which the LORD sware unto thy fathers to give thee.

The LORD shall open unto thee His good treasure, the Heaven to give the rain unto thy land in his season, and to bless all the work of thine hand: and thou shalt lend unto many nations, and thou shalt not borrow.

And the LORD shall make thee the head, and not the tail; and thou shalt be above only, and thou shalt not be beneath; if that thou hearken unto the commandments of the LORD thy God, which I command thee this day, to observe and to do them:

And thou shalt not go aside from any of the words which I command thee this day, to the right hand, or to the left, to go after other gods to serve them." (KJV)

Which is Greater?

The Power of the Curse or.....   The Power of the Blessing ?

"For if by one man's (Adam) **offence death reigned by one, MUCH MORE they which receive abundance of grace and of the gift of righteousness SHALL REIGN IN LIFE by one, Jesus Christ.   Therefore as by the offence of one judgment came upon all men to condemnation; even so by the righteousness of One** (Jesus) **the free gift came upon all men unto justification of life. For as by one man's disobedience many were made sinners, SO BY THE OBEDIENCE OF ONE SHALL MANY BE MADE RIGHTEOUS." Rom. 5:17-19 (KJV)**

For if by the sin of Adam all mankind was cursed, how MUCH MORE shall we be blessed when the second Adam (Jesus) comes and obeys? Think about it, which is more powerful?   Is the sin and destruction that came upon the earth by Adam's disobedience more potent? Or, should the righteousness and grace that came upon the earth by Jesus' obedience be able to obliterate the destruction? What Jesus did is MUCH MORE powerful!! The blessing of Abraham, that has now been given to the children of the Promise (Jewish and Gentile people who believe in God's Messiah – Jesus Christ), is infinitely more powerful than the curse of Adam.

He has made everything new.   The fallen world no longer is the "real world," for the Kingdom of Heaven is now here.   As new creations...we are already residents in the Kingdom of Heaven on earth, if indeed we seek shelter under the shadow of the Almighty.   We are in a new reality, and a new economy. In the contest for power, darkness cannot overwhelm even the small light of a simple candle. One tiny light can overwhelm the deepest darkness.   What then of the omnipotent power of our Lord Jesus Christ?

Man's authority over the earth has never been denied, nor has it been put into question. Here, do this: Find in the scriptures where the authority of Adam and those who followed was withdrawn by God.   Then, find where satan was given authority over the earth. You will not be able to find references to these, for neither exists. The world is in the condition it is in because WE are in charge.   All the evil that exists upon the earth, is only able to do so for the lack of someone who will exercise their authority to put a stop to it.

It's a lot like the wild, wild west.   There is no law and order because there is no sheriff. We are all looking over our shoulder, hoping God will do something about the evil. He HAS done something! He has appointed us as the stewards and guardians of the earth. Despite all the consequences of our complacency, He will not usurp our authority until the end of time. Remember, "all that is necessary for evil to prevail in this world is for good people (God's People) to do nothing." And that dear brothers and sisters is why evil reigns.

Evil reigns because we do nothing. The reason our loved ones suffer and die, the reason the enemy wanders about the earth stealing, killing, and destroying, is because we all content ourselves with being civilians amidst the greatest war of all time. When we had the choice to make, we did not choose very well where to invest our lives. We are daily caught unprepared before an unmerciful adversary. Our loved ones are taken, and we blame God. But God has provided us everything necessary to be more than conquerors. <u>Despite this, we have become nothing more than pitiful and pathetic misrepresentations of what we were created to be</u>.

"Submit yourselves therefore to God. Resist the devil, and he will flee from you." **James 4:7 (KJV)**

As long as people buy into the notion that suffering comes from God, we will not resist, and we will embrace it or at the least tolerate it. And since the truth is that the devil is the destroyer and not God, if we do not resist him, then there is nothing to stop him. My question is: If suffering comes from God, and it's His will for you to do so.... then why do you ever pray for people in the first place? Are you not praying against His Will? And if it's His will, then please explain to me why you do not pray for more suffering for you and your loved ones? If you want what God wants, then you want as much suffering as you can get, right? Quite frankly, with that reasoning, then it would probably mean that the more deadly the better, right?

"Verily I say unto you, 'Whatsoever ye shall bind (forbid) **on earth shall be bound** (forbidden) **in Heaven** (by Me)**; and whatsoever ye shall loose** (permit) **on earth shall be loosed** (permitted) **in Heaven** (by Me)."**

Matthew 18:18-20 (KJV)

But He has left it up to us to decide what happens on earth. God will not force healing upon us. If we will tolerate (loose/allow) illness and injury, so will He. That means if we entertain the thought that illness is inevitable, and consider that it is "our lot in this fallen world," if even for just a brief period of time, then it becomes ours.

If we give it an inch, believe me… it will take a mile. If we will stand up against (bind, restrain, resist) it, then so will He. Therefore, if a man chooses to believe God won't heal him, God will not usurp that man's authority to deny himself healing. God does not usurp the authority of man to choose his own way. Come heck or high water, come life or death, we are the captain of our own ship, and our tongue is the rudder. Whatever we say, goes! We have the authority. Good, bad, or indifferent, we are the sum total of the words we choose to describe our lives. For what comes from our lips pours from the abundance of our heart. If we have a heart filled with belief, we shall have the reward of belief. If it is full of unbelief, then we shall suffer the consequences of unbelief.

Often I hear Christian brothers and sisters referring to their conditions in possessive terms. It always makes me cringe. "My headache, my MS, my diabetes, my flu, my cancer, my any kind of condition you can possibly imagine." I never, ever, ever lay claim to any condition that I did not request. If I did not order it, I don't want it. It always gets stamped "Return to Sender." Now symptomatic temptations do fall upon me at times, however they are not mine. After all, we are guaranteed that in this life we will have troubles, however…we should be of good cheer, because He has overcome them all (at the cross)! Headaches are never mine. They are attacks against me, and against the Will and Word of God. They are trespassers and have no place in me. I rebuke them and reject them at the door, lest they get a foothold in my life.

And finally, regarding faith: In this world, God has the power and you have the authority (delegated to you by Him who possesses the power to enforce it). As long as one walks outside of faith, he only has the limited power he himself is capable of generating as a human being. For most of us, that's not very much. We must all agree that some people seem to have a great deal more power and influence than other people do. Nevertheless, even the most powerful people throughout history at their very best (or worst for that matter!) were altogether powerless, and temporary. What of Solomon? Have you ever read the laments of this great man in the book of Ecclesiastes? What about a man though, who relinquishes command of his life to his creator for the pursuit of an eternal kingdom? What would happen if the Lord found a humble man He could flow all His power through? If this were conceivable, how much power would that man possess? That is, if His limitations were whatever God's limitations are?

"By faith Abraham, when he was called, obeyed to go out unto a place which he was to receive for an inheritance; and he went out, not knowing whither he went. By faith he became a sojourner in the land of promise, as in a land not his own, dwelling in tents, with Isaac and Jacob, the heirs with him of the same promise: having taken up his abode in tents <u>for he looked for the city which hath the foundations, whose builder and maker is God.</u>"

Hebrews 11:8-10 (ASV)

"...let him ask in faith without any doubting, for the one who doubts is like the surf of the sea driven and tossed by the wind. For let not that man expect that he will receive anything from the Lord, being a double-minded man, unstable in all his ways." James 1:6-8 (NASB)

We are in partnership with God, even if we refuse to believe it or agree to it. Why does it say "if a man doubts while praying he should not expect he will receive anything of the Lord; because he is an unstable man?" How does our doubting have anything to do with the result? Here it is. God has already made the first move. He gave His Word, and the promises written in it. Like eternal salvation, they are a done deal. However, just like the salvation of our souls, the promises for this life are not ours until we act in faith to confess them with our mouths, in order to receive them as our own.

"...if you confess with your mouth Jesus as Lord, and believe in your heart that God raised Him from the dead, you shall be saved; for with the heart man believes resulting in righteousness, and with the mouth he confesses, resulting in salvation. For the Scripture says, 'Whoever believes in Him will not be disappointed." Romans 10:9-10 (NASB)

For the promise of healing to manifest itself, one must do their part. Our part, is to eradicate evil unbelief from our heart and confess with our mouth the truth of His promises. In order to take salvation as our own, we must believe with our heart and speak with our mouth, with no doubt. Taking ownership of His promises are no different. I was told years ago, "Ryker, you are not going to get from God what you want, you are only going to get what you expect." That's what this scripture in James is saying.

When God makes a promise, there is no question, He will keep it. <u>That's why He makes promises, so He can keep them.</u> Frequently in these visions, you will see God instructing me to do my part. You will also see me respond. And unfortunately, you will also see what happens when I allow doubt to creep in from time to time, as well.

"...and this is the confidence which we have before Him, that, if we ask anything according to His will, He hears us. And if we know that He hears us in whatever we ask, WE KNOW THAT WE HAVE the requests which we have asked from Him."   **1 John 5:14 (NASB)**

The following statement is necessary before moving on.: Everything about God is FAITH. And, I do mean EVERYTHING. It is so much so, that if what we are doing to serve Him does not require faith of us, then it is probably not coming from Him.

Now, let me ask you a question.   Which has the greater faith? Is it the one who <u>BELIEVES</u> what God <u>CAN</u> do? Or, is it the one who <u>KNOWS</u> what God <u>WILL</u> do?Even the demons believe in what God can do. Looking around at creation itself, tells us what God can do. But, how often do we pray with expectation concerning what God <u>WILL</u> do? How can anyone pray without doubting, if we don't know what God will do? If a person has no idea what God will do, then it impossible to not have doubt. All such prayers are merely hoping. Hoping and wishing are not the same thing as faith. Faith KNOWS!!! Faith knows that God is a GOOD God, and always wants to bless us with abundant life.   Hoping implies uncertainty and doubt about His goodness. If we are merely hoping we are saved. we are in danger of hell both in this world and the one to come.

We have to do our part. We have to do what Romans 10:9-10 said about salvation. <u>We have to believe it, and speak it</u>. Again, as this Scripture reflects, it is inadequate to believe in our heart that Jesus is God. To receive Him, as our Savior, we have to speak it with our mouth as well. So it is, when we receive healing or any other answer to prayer. We have to believe it with our heart, and confess it with our mouth. Otherwise, it will remain a "great big uncertain maybe" in our life.

"Now faith is THE SUBSTANCE OF THINGS HOPED FOR, the evidence of things NOT (yet) SEEN. For by it the elders obtained a good report. Through faith we understand that the worlds were framed by the Word of God, so that the things which are seen were not made of things which do appear."

Hebrews 11:1-3 (NASB)

Why, and how does faith work?

All matter that exists is made of faith. Every single molecule, every atom, everything that was ever created is made of faith. Again for emphasis, faith is the building block of all that exists. It is the substance of all that God spoke out of the abundance of His heart. Therefore, it should not surprise us that everything in creation responds to faith! Faith is what substance is made of. Let's use an illustration. The most common component of our physical life is water. We are made mostly of water. Take water away from us, and very quickly our body would break down and die. Restore water to us though, and our body will quickly respond. It responds to that which it is made of.

Tolerating Contradictions: It is very difficult to sum together the whole of scripture on the matter of healing in a brief manner. However at this early stage, as mentioned previously, if basic understanding is not presented, most of what follows will make little sense. Here is how to sum up the issue of healing: Healing is nothing more than eliminating contradictions to God's Word which have manifested themselves in our bodies. Healing is simply the process of bringing our bodies into agreement with the Word of God concerning them.

Our bodies, and all of creation, were designed in absolute perfection. All the bad, evil, illness, injury, and corruption existing in the world does so in contradiction to the Word of God concerning it. We were not made to be cursed. We were made to be blessed. It was the introduction of sin into the world that invited corruption. The obedience of Christ, on the other hand, invited grace. All of the contradictions to God's Word exist as the direct result of the curse. Through the completed work of Christ in us though, we are no longer subject to the curse.

"For Christ also hath once suffered for sins, the just for the unjust, that He might bring us to God..."   **1 Peter 3:18 (KJV)**

~ 56 ~

What is Grace?

Most are of the opinion that grace is defined as "unmerited favor." While this is not necessarily false, it by no means captures or defines the fullness of grace. Look at it this way. Exactly what do we deserve in the great scheme of things? One thing, and one thing only: death. On this basis then, if God were to give me a broken pencil or a half-eaten apple, would this then not also be grace? This definition by no means defines grace. Here is a better definition.

"I am crucified with Christ: nevertheless I live; yet not I, but Christ liveth in me: and the life which I now live in the flesh I live by the faith of the Son of God, who loved me, and gave Himself for me." Galatians 2:20 (KJV)

"And if children, then heirs; heirs of God, and joint-heirs with Christ."

Romans 8:17 (KJV)

The life we live now is in the righteousness of Christ, and not our own. Our own was hung on the cross with Christ. Therefore grace is: "receiving everything Jesus deserves." We live by grace (if we walk with God). This grace is the result of our unrighteousness being wholly exchanged for His righteousness, as referred to in I Peter 3:18 above. The fact is, in Christ we ARE Christ. He is the head, we are the body. Together we are Him. Just as much as a husband and wife are One, both as a legal entity and in the spiritual realm. In John 9:5 Jesus says, "While I am in the world, I am the light of the world." In Him, we are Him. In this world, we are now the light of the world and the salt of the earth.

"You are the light of the world. A city that is set on a hill cannot be hid.

Matthew 5:14 (NASB)

This is all a mere matter of submission, when it gets right down to it. There are two cornerstone laws a Christian has available to choose from. There is the law of Nature, and the Law of the Spirit. We therefore have two Lords to choose from. Another way to look at it is as follows: We can either live according to the law of fate, or the law of faith. To live by the law of fate means we live by averages, luck, fortune, and the idea that "whatever will be, will be." How many times have you heard Christians climb on an airplane with these words, "Well, if it's my time to go, then it's my time to go! There is nothing I can do about it." This statement is very unscriptural and has caused many an early death. These are words of fate, not faith.

Almost all Christians live by fate. They have no choice, for they do not know their God intimately. They have no idea what to expect from Him. Why? Because they do not spend time with Him, and they don't know His Word. If they do know it, they don't believe it. And if they believe it, they find a way to excuse themselves from it. They believe He is unknowable and unpredictable. In this way, their God is no different than allah. Whatever happens to us, good or bad, must be the will of allah. On this basis, a Christian who lives by fate is as subject to the same laws of fate/nature, as are his lost neighbors. The Christian who lives by the law of faith/spirit though, sees a whole different paradigm, because the law of faith/spirit supersedes the law of fate/nature; for those who walk in it.

Imagine being in the military and having a military officer from a foreign country giving you orders. Would you recognize his authority to send you into harm's way? If your commanding officer instructed you to follow the orders of that foreign officer, then yes you should recognize that authority. But, God has given no such orders to you; in regard to the devil.

"Submit yourselves therefore to God. Resist the devil, and he will flee from you. Draw nigh to God and He will draw nigh to you. Cleanse your hands, ye sinners; and purify your hearts, you double minded"   **James 4:7-8 (KJV)**

In this same way, we should only recognize the law (authority) of the spirit over our person. Therefore when the law of the flesh, nature, fate (no matter which way you want to describe it) comes knocking on your door, tempting you to believe the worst; do not tolerate it. <u>Verbally</u> rebuke it in Jesus name. We are under no obligation to recognize or obey the commands and threats of this foreign authority. We should only bend our knee to one King. We should never be double minded about our allegiances. If a threat is received from the natural world, like "you are going to die of cancer;" refuse it. Do not recognize the authority of cancer over your body. Only bend your knee to one King. Him who says, "you shall live and not die."

On this basis, any illness, injury, or lack that is imposed upon you or those you cover is <u>ABSOLUTELY against the will of God</u>. Any such threat is a trespasser against the Kingdom of Heaven. Therefore an attack against you is an attack against the Kingdom of God, and an attack against the Kingdom of God is an attack against

Jesus, and an attack against Jesus is an attack against God Himself. It should therefore be dealt with as such.

"...And from the days of John the Baptist (who represents the last of the old order of things since Adam) **until now the Kingdom of Heaven suffereth violence, and THE** (spiritually) **VIOLENT TAKE IT** (back) **BY FORCE."**

Matthew 11:12 (KJV)

Now it is a very difficult to reprogram our previous mindset. As humans, it's natural for us to only believe what we see. It's natural to tend toward the negative. It's natural to want to take the easy path. But, if you want your inheritance, you're going to have to fight for it, just like the Israelites fought for their Promised Land. Let's not forget God's instructions to them. That is, to take it by force. They were ordered to kill everything that drew breath, men, women, children, even the animals, everything. While God delivered their enemies into their hands, they still fought the fight in almost every case.

"For those who are (living) **according to the flesh SET THEIR MINDS on the things of the flesh** (meaning, the natural world, which is only available to be seen by the five senses)**, but those who are** (living) **according to the Spirit, the things of the Spirit. FOR THE MIND SET ON THE FLESH IS DEATH, but THE MIND SET ON THE SPIRIT IS LIFE AND PEACE. Because the mind set on the flesh is hostile toward God; for it does not subject itself to the law of God, for it is not even able to do so; and THOSE WHO ARE IN THE FLESH CANNOT PLEASE GOD.**

However, YOU ARE NOT IN THE FLESH, but in the Spirit, if indeed the Spirit of God dwells in you. But if anyone does not have the Spirit of Christ, He does not belong to Him. And if Christ is in you, though the body is dead because of sin, yet the spirit is alive because of righteousness. BUT IF THE SPIRIT OF HIM WHO RAISED JESUS FROM THE DEAD DWELLS IN YOU, HE WHO RAISED CHRIST JESUS FROM THE DEAD WILL ALSO GIVE LIFE TO YOUR MORTAL BODIES, through His Spirit who indwells you.

So then, brethren, WE ARE UNDER OBLIGATION, NOT TO THE FLESH TO LIVE ACCORDING TO THE FLESH, for if you are living according to the flesh, YOU MUST DIE; but if by the Spirit you are putting to death the deeds of the body YOU WILL LIVE."   **Romans 8:5-13 (NASB)**

"Finally, my breathren, be STRONG IN THE LORD, and IN THE POWER OF HIS MIGHT. Put on the whole armor of God, that YE MAY BE ABLE TO STAND

AGAINST THE WILES OF THE DEVIL, for we wrestle not against flesh and blood, but against principalities, against powers, against the rulers of the darkness in this world, against spiritual wickedness in high places."

Ephesians 6:10-12 (KJV)

"The WEAPONS of OUR WARFARE are not carnal, but MIGHTY through God to the PULLING DOWN of STRONGHOLDS; CASTING DOWN IMAGINATIONS, and every HIGH THING that exalteth itself against the KNOWLEDGE of God, and BRINGING INTO CAPTIVITY every thought to the OBEDIENCE of Christ; and having in all readiness to revenge all disobedience, WHEN YOUR OBEDIENCE IS FULFILLED."   2 Corinthians 10:4-6 (KJV)

"Death and Life are in THE POWER OF THE TONGUE: and they that love it shall eat the fruit thereof."   Proverbs 18:21 (KJV)

"I call Heaven and earth to record this day against you, that I HAVE SET BEFORE YOU LIFE AND DEATH, BLESSING, AND CURSING: THEREFORE CHOOSE LIFE., THAT BOTH THOU AND THY SEED MAY LIVE. That thou mayest love the Lord thy God, and that thou mayest obey His voice, and that thou mayest cleave unto Him: FOR HE IS THY LIFE, AND THE LENGTH OF THY DAYS."   Deuteronomy 30:19-20 (KJV)

Either way, we get to choose. Life and death are in the power of our tongue. Therefore, turn to your adversary and declare "I am a child of the King, and as such, I do not recognize your power or authority over me; nor anything that is mine. You are trespassing on God's Kingdom, and you WILL be dealt with accordingly."

Here is the thing. It has to get all the way inside us, and become a part of us. If we tolerate ANY contradiction with the Word of God, as it pertains to our lives, those we love, or the things that are ours, then so will God. But if you call those contradictions what they are and stand against them, so will God.

"Verily I say unto you, "Whatsoever ye shall bind (forbid) on earth shall be bound (forbidden) in Heaven (by Me): and whatsoever ye shall loose (permit) on earth shall be loosed (permitted) in Heaven (by Me)."   Matt. 18:18 (KJV)

Clearing the Path

Throughout history there have been many Daniel Boones, Davy Crockets and other Trail Blazers. These adventurers not only risked it all to go where no one had gone before, but they blazed trails for others to follow as well. They inspired people with stories of high adventure and grand opportunity. They realized how empty even the most awe-inspiring experiences of life can be, if one does not share them with others. The world needs more of this breed of people. So, it's not surprising that the Lord should instruct me to break a path to my secret place and write this book.

Nor is it difficult to imagine what His instruction to "clear that path" represents. Remember, the path represents the path to the truth. What is the truth obscured by? Lies and half-truths, simple as that. These lies and half-truths are not merely the ones fed to me, personally. They have been fed to everyone for thousands of years. We just spent some time talking about healing. How many lies and half-truths are being taught, from pulpits, about this one topic?

It's easy to remember when my path clearing started in earnest. The process began in 2001. It was that year God sent the first man to shake me up. It was not until 2003 though, that I came to terms with how pervasive my faulty understanding was. By that time, being able to tell what was sound and what was rotten had become extremely difficult. On the outside, they looked the same.

It was like trying to remove and replace the studs in a house, which were eaten up by termites and decay. Many of them were load bearing and the damage was very extensive. The only way the restoration could be completed; was by disassembling the entire structure and rebuilding it from the ground up. This took a full year of hearing the Word every day, and dissecting it piece by piece. By the time the project was finished, it had become, for all practical purposes, an entirely new house. It only looked the same on the outside. There are numerous allusions to this process reflected in the visions to follow.

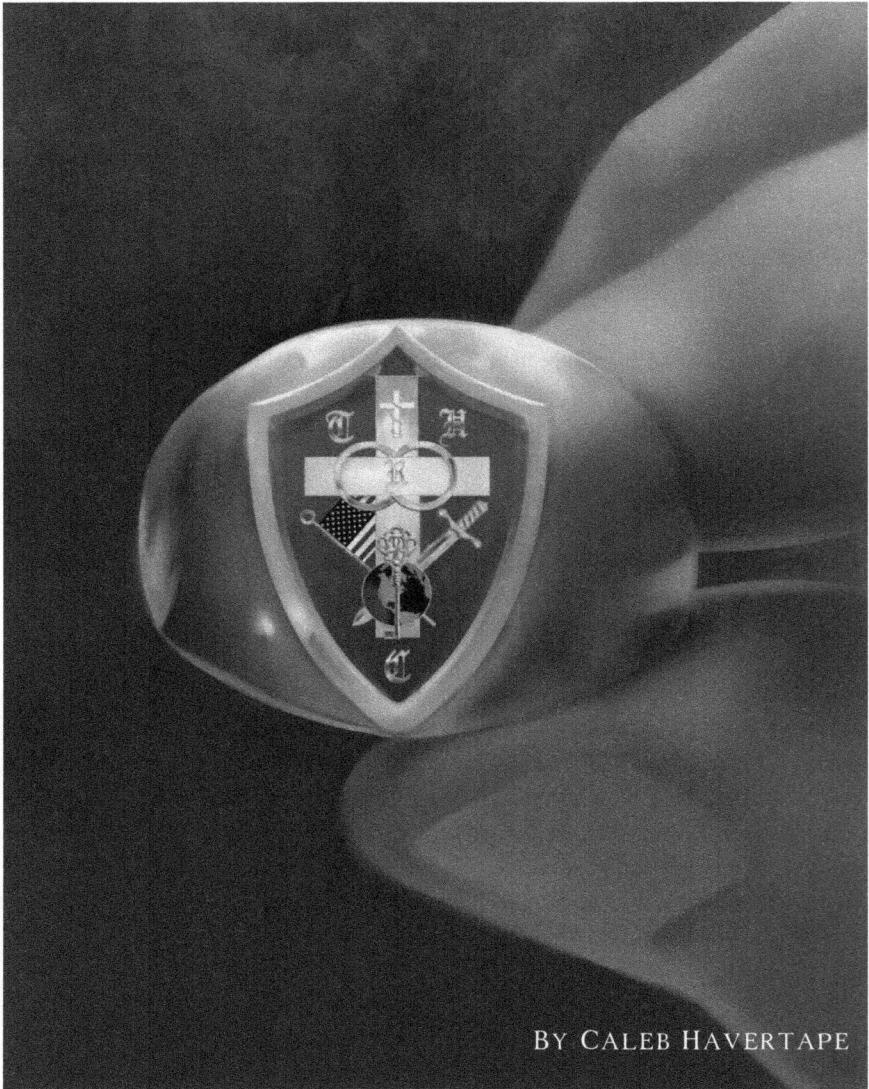

By Caleb Havertape

Chapter Three

THE RING

The very next day, I returned to meet the Lord in the middle of the night. This time, it was with determination to start fixing up the place. The wind was blowing fiercely outside, so sitting on the sofa seemed preferable. Once there, I relaxed and began imagining the path to the secret place again. After only a few moments, it opened up before me.

I found myself vigorously swinging a machete, in the act of clearing willow branches, tree limbs, and vines from the path. The arduous work went on for a couple hours, as a rough trail to the secret place began to take shape. Eventually, the fresh cut path broke open to the clearing. Finally laying eyes on the chapel, it was pleasing to see nothing had changed for the worse this time.

Once again Jesus met me at the top of the steps, and led me through the doorway.   When we stepped inside, He said there was something He'd like to give me. With that, He began walking along the right side of the room. As He did, He ran His outstretched right hand along the row of enclaves (like you would run your hand along a fence line while walking beside it). The thumping of His fingers, as they ran over the ornate wood carving and the edges of the cabinets, was clearly audible. When He got to the first corner, He turned left and continued along that line of enclaves. When He got to one in the middle of that wall, He stopped.

Taking hold of the door handle, He turned to me and spoke in a hushed voice. "This is not what we spoke about last time (headaches), but it is what I'd like to give you today. When He opened the door, white light spilled out with near blinding brilliance. Inside, a small shelf could be seen at about eye level.

Reaching inside, He took hold of a small object and presented it to me. As I extended my hand, He dropped it into my palm. It was a gold signet ring. Shifting the ring from side to side, it glimmered brightly against the radiating sunlight from the holes in the roof. Looking more intently at it, I was most pleased to see its crest bore the coat of arms He had inspired me to create for my family some years ago.

He explained that the ring was a gift from Him. It was considered a symbol of His power and authority appointed to me and my family. Furthermore, He said, "This ring bears the seal which tells the spiritual world you represent me and My Kingdom on earth. If you say something is so, it is so. If there is anything you need or desire, present this ring and have it put on my account." With that, He took hold of the ring and slid it on my right hand ring finger. With a smile, I expressed my appreciation for such a special gift.

With my head, it was easy to understand that this was an incredible blessing. With my heart though, it was difficult to fathom the depth of it. Clearly, there would be a great deal to learn about this moment. My reply was a simple, "Thank you," and assurance of my return the next evening.

PERSONAL COMMENTARY

The Clearing Tool Metaphors

There are a few tools that are useful when breaking trail. Some of these were used during the visions to break and improve the trail to my secret place. Here is a small list of them:

Machete: For those who don't already know, a machete is a single bladed knife about 2-3 feet long. It is designed for clearing paths through dense weeds and brush. It is used primarily in a side to side swinging motion. It may also be used in a chopping motion on limbs, vines, and saplings. While it might ease the passage through dense vegetation, it does not necessarily leave anything but a crude path behind it. Its purpose is not for creating a permanent trail. Rather, it is to get from one place to the other through otherwise impassable vegetation.

What does the machete represent?

While a machete is not a very elegant tool, it is very effective at making passage possible. In the beginning of this process of clearing things out of my life; all that was necessary was to be able to get back to meet the Lord. The finer details were just not as important. It seemed more prudent to question everything and clear anything that blocked my advance.

The thought reminds me of the day I received the Baptism of the Holy Spirit. On that day, I had gone forward at the end of the church service. After the crowd finally dispersed, I stepped up to the pastor and said, "everything you just described about what it is like to NOT have the baptism of the Holy Spirit fits me perfectly, for there is no power in anything I try to accomplish. I was raised in a church which taught people who believe like you do - are from the devil. But, I have been delivered of that blasphemy against the Holy Spirit. And now, even though I don't understand everything you have been teaching, I want to receive the Baptism of the Holy Spirit with all my heart."

He excitedly told me how great this was, and that I should come forward after church next Sunday. Stopping him, I said, "Pastor you don't understand. I'm not leaving here without the baptism of the Holy Spirit! I refuse to take another step without Him flowing through me, as you described. It's been horrible for us without His power in our lives. We need Him today!" Somewhat startled, he said, "Well, uhmm, uh, can you wait here while I go see if I can catch the elders before they leave?" "Of course," I said. With that, he rushed off to assemble his helpers.

That day set a whole new course for me and my family. My past teachings were screaming at me to sit down and shut up. But I refused to listen anymore and ran headlong into faith. I had already lived the fruit of the past and it tasted awful. I had tasted the Lord now, and He tasted good. Whack, Whack, Whack, I found my way home again.

Chainsaw: We have two of them. They are perfect tools for cutting trees and heavier brush. There is one (Stihl) suitable for large trees. And another much smaller one (el cheapo), for small trees and brush. The Stihl was used for cutting and clearing the fallen trees lying across the path. The smaller one was used for the smaller trees and brush that loppers could not cut through. The disadvantage is that chainsaws are heavy, noisy, and the vibration wears a person out. Chainsaws are also prone to kick back, particularly when dealing with brush. This makes them very dangerous. But, as they say back home in Montana... "Chainsaws Rule."

What does the chainsaw represent?

Naturally the large logs, trees, and well established brush on the path represent the large doctrinal lies and half-truths. The major lies I had been swallowing for years, only the awesome "Stihl," chainsaw could cut through those. (By the way, I am not getting any sponsorship from Stihl for this product placement, I am just a big fan). The biggest fallen logs in my life were the ones that said, "God is responsible for all the evil in my life, and He means well by treating me badly." Our pastor took a chainsaw to those logs every Sunday when he began his message with:

"The thief comes, but for to steal, to kill, and to destroy. But, I come that you might have life, and have it abundantly." John 10:10 (NASB)

One day our pastor asked, "Do you have any idea what the state would do to you; if you did to your children what people accuse God of doing to His? They would take your children away and throw you in prison. How is it possible, that what would be unthinkable for you is perfectly acceptable for God? Why is it wrong for you to abuse your children, but not wrong for God? If killing, maiming, and stealing from His children is ok for God, what makes it wrong for us? Is it possible to hold ourselves to a higher standard than God holds Himself?" Then He would quote:

"If ye then, being evil, know how to give good gifts unto your children, how much more shall your Father which is in Heaven give good things to them that ask Him." **Matthew 7:11 (KJV)**

Every time we sat down in that church, we could hear the chainsaws roaring to life. Still, it took quite some time for the old mindset to be cut out. Believe me... it took a whole year of basically the same sermon every Sunday!

Loppers: This tool is a pair of shears with handles about eighteen inches long. They are designed to easily cut through limbs up to about two inches thick. One would find them to be a more detailed type tool, primarily intended for pruning fruit trees. However for trails, with overhanging branches, intruding limbs, and exposed roots they are also the perfect tool.

What do the loppers represent?

The best tool for cutting through lies is the truth. Now that we were eagerly consuming the Word of God, it meant every day an old lie was being lopped off. Once the chainsaws cleared our understanding, the lopping action became constant and earnest. The Bible literally sprang to life! Best of all, it began to make absolute sense. Everything went together like a perfectly fitted puzzle. Understanding cleared our confusion, questions, and uncertainties like the morning sun does to a hanging fog. God's Word had become living and active like never before. It was thrilling to read again. After leading others for all those years, finally my own questions and uncertainties were being answered. It was, and remains to this day, to be the most exciting time of my life.

Years later, the lies of the past are still be lopped off every time I open God's Word. *The tough thing about understanding God's Word is that we do so based upon what we already know. And often what we know is wrong. Therefore anything laid upon that foundation also becomes wrong. The better part of humility is required, in order to start over. Unfortunately, there are very few who would not hold to their precious opinions even to the death.*

"But no one puts a patch of unshrunk cloth on an old garment; for the patch pulls away from the garment, and a worse tear results. Nor do men put new wine into old wineskins; otherwise the wineskins burst, and the wine pours out, and the wineskins are ruined; but they put new wine into fresh wineskins, and both are preserved." **Matthew 9:16-17 (NASB)**

Shovel: Shovels are a common hand tool for digging dirt with. For breaking trail, it is an essential tool for digging up rocks and roots. Of course, it is also instrumental in creating nice smooth pathways unobstructed by natural trip hazards.

What does the shovel represent ?

Anyone who knows anything about gardening or landscaping knows if you don't get the roots, vegetation will grow back. Furthermore, it's the roots and rocks buried in our paths that trip us and cause us to stumble the most. This is where a shovel comes in handy. After all the overhanging obstructions, fallen trees, and brush were cleared out of the way, attention was turned to digging into my understanding. In the process, many rocks and roots were dug up and discarded.

"Study to shew thyself approved unto God, a workman that needeth not to be ashamed, rightly dividing the Word of Truth." **2 Timothy 2:15 (KJV)**

Rake: Once the rocks, roots, and other debris are removed from the surface of a path, rakes become very useful. It is perfect for removing leaves, limbs, and other small pieces of vegetative debris. In addition, it does very well at smoothing out the surface of the path.

What does the rake represent ?

The clearing process leaves a great deal of debris, dirt, and holes in the path. This is where a rake makes all the difference. The rake was useful for clearing leftover debris, filling in holes, and smoothing out the path. Intimacy with God is like that rake, and has all the benefits. Our Lord is chief encourager, best friend, and confidant. When there are questions, He has answers. When confused, He unravels the tangled weave of our understanding. He comforts, consoles, and leads us on our way so that our path is made straight. It is He that smoothed my path for me, and made it a pleasure to walk upon. There were also things that needed to be removed from "self," such as pride. He helped me get these obstacles out of the way. Because of this, the smoothing process also enables others to want to walk on this same path.

"Trust in the Lord with all thine heart; and lean not unto thine own understanding. In all thy ways acknowledge Him, and He shall direct thy paths." Proverbs 3:5-6 (KJV)

The Ring:

Anyone who knows the scriptures knows this truth about the Lord, He uses symbols frequently to convey His messages in the most meaningful way possible. Whether it is Moses' staff, the sword, the shield, or the very cross itself, He means for us to get the message, and then act in faith upon it.

In Jesus day, a signet ring was significant. The signet ring of a king bore his crest and only he and his rightful heirs to the throne possessed it. When he made a legal declaration or correspondence, a bit of wax would be used to seal the document and it would be stamped with his ring so that it bore his crest. Though we don't wear rings for this purpose anymore, we still sign documents with our signature to serve the same purpose.

Bearing God's signet ring tells the spiritual world that we are heirs to His throne. As such, we have the same power, authority, and resources of the King. We are second only to the King Himself. The Scriptures say that Jesus is the King of kings, and the Lord of lords. The fact that we are adopted and grafted into His family makes no difference whatsoever. A challenge or threat against us, as His royal family, is a challenge and a threat against the High King. It is a treasonable offense, and quite dangerous to the attacker's wellbeing.

For me in particular, this ring plays a significant role in defining who we are as a family. During medieval times each family had a specially designed coat of arms reflecting something significant about their family. It was passed down from generation to generation. When my wife and I purposed to start over as a family, and chart a new destiny before God, He inspired us to craft a coat of arms. The crest shown in this vision was the ultimate result. This coat of arms allowed me to understand what it would forever mean for my family to carry His name.

Each element in our crest carries with it symbolic significance. Its shape reflects that of a shield; the shield of faith to be exact. At the center of the shield there is the cross of our Savior, upon which everything else hangs. At its three corners are the letters, T, H, and C. These represent Truth, Honor, and Courage. At the head of the cross is another cross upon which hangs a serpent. This represents healing as symbolized by the serpent on the staff that Moses bore for healing those of Israel who looked upon it in the wilderness. (Which itself was a symbol of our suffering and death that the devil/serpent brings being destroyed on the cross with Christ. For, by His stripes, we are healed). Wrapped around the center of the cross are two interlocked rings. These represent marriage. Inside them is the letter "K" for Kern, our last name. This represents family. At the foot of the cross is the Earth with a Key over it. This represents the keys to the Kingdom of Heaven, on the Earth. And behind the world is our flag and a sword. These represent our service to freedom both in God and Country.

It must be said, there is no "power" in the ring itself any more than there was in Moses' staff. It is simply a symbol. However, when used in faith it allows God to exercise His power over the natural world through us in a dramatic way.

"And Jesus came and spake saying, All Power is given unto me in Heaven and Earth. Go ye therefore and teach all nations." **Matthew 28:18 (KJV)**

"For the Son of Man (Jesus) is as a man taking a far journey, who left His house, and GAVE AUTHORITY to His servants, and to every man His work, and commanded the porter to watch." **Mark 13:34 (KJV)**

"BEHOLD, I GIVE UNTO YOU POWER to Tred on Serpents and Scorpions, and Over ALL the power of the enemy and NOTHING shall by any means hurt you." **Luke 10:19 (KJV)**

"Verily, Verily, I say unto you, 'If you BELIEVE on Me the works that I do shall you do also AND Greater Works Than These SHALL YOU DO, because I go to the Father." **John 14:12-13 (KJV)**

"I will give you the KEYS of the KINGDOM of HEAVEN; and WHATEVER you shall bind on earth SHALL be bound in Heaven, and whatever you shall loose on earth shall be loosed in Heaven." Matt. 16:19 (KJV)

"In righteousness you will be ESTABLISHED; you will be FAR FROM OPPRESSION, and you will not fear; and from terror, for IT WILL NOT COME NEAR YOU. If anyone assails you IT WILL NOT BE FROM ME. Whoever assails you WILL FALL BECAUSE OF YOU. Behold, I Myself have created the smith who blows the fire of coals, and brings out a weapon for its work; and I have created the destroyer to ruin. NO WEAPON that is formed against you shall prosper; and every tongue that accuses you in judgment you will condemn. THIS IS THE HERITAGE OF THE SERVANTS OF THE LORD, and their vindication is from me declares the Lord." Isaiah 54:14-17 (KJV)

"And the Lord shall MAKE THEE THE HEAD, AND NOT THE TAIL; and THOU SHALT BE ABOVE ONLY, AND THOU SHALT NOT BE BENEATH; if that thou hearken unto the commandments of the Lord thy God, which I command thee this day, to observe and to do them." Deuteronomy 28:13 (KJV)

"But my God shall supply ALL your need <u>ACCORDING to His RICHES</u> in glory by Christ Jesus." Ephesians 4:19 (KJV)

"You will be made rich in every way so that you can be generous on every occasion, and through us your generosity will result in thanksgiving to God."

2 Corinthians 9:11 (NIV)

"Now unto Him that is able to do exceeding abundantly above all that we ask or think, according to the power that worketh in us, Unto Him be glory in the church by Christ Jesus throughout all ages, world without end. Amen."

Ephesians 3:20-21 (NIV)

Do you believe these Scriptures? The first most important thing we can do to get the truth into our life, is to clear a path for it. Once we have done that, we learn God's provision is something He has already made available to us. We should trust Him for it, and not entertain doubt about His sincerity. We can also learn from this vision that we are not all by ourselves. Remember, it is only our "self" who can hold back

His blessings. We do so through doubt and unbelief.   God says what He means, and means what He says, and so should we. If He says He will provide, we should treat Him as if He never lies and never exaggerates.

We don't get out of our relationship with God what we want, we get what we expect. So, we have to change our expectations. We should expect a great deal from God because He offers a great deal.   If I ever found out I expect too much of my God, I would most certainly seek a greater God than He. My God will be one who is bigger than my expectations. God makes promises so He can keep them. Furthermore, He is NOT an Indian giver. For those that are not sure about God, they can be sure not to expect anything. They are unstable people full of unbelief. As for me, I have no doubts that My God, IS God.

"But he must ask in faith without doubting, for the one who doubts is like the surf of the sea, driven and tossed by the wind. For that man ought not to expect that he will receive anything from the Lord, being a double-minded man unstable in all his ways."   **James 1:6-8 (NASB)**

Living Water

By Caleb Havertape

Chapter Four

LIVING WATER

"And those from among you will rebuild the Ancient Ruins; you will raise up the age-old foundations; And you will be called the Repairer of the Breach, The Restorer of the streets in which to dwell."   **Isaiah 58:12   (NASB)**

One night, just before bedtime, the Lord told me to "come outside later." Awaking around 2:30 a.m. I went outside, as instructed. Seated on the hill a few moments later, I asked the Lord if I could go back to my secret place. He replied, "Yes, let's do that first. When we are done though, let us go stand in the North Gate."

This was agreeable. So picking up where I left off last time, I resumed clearing brush.   During this effort, a discovery was made that I had not realized before. Underneath all the vegetation, was an old road bed. As I was standing there contemplating this realization, Jesus appeared. Taking no note of my discovery, He said, "You have done well with the trail. Might I suggest you let me bring in a bulldozer for the rest of this project? Why don't you work on the vines that cover the outer walls of the chapel? When you get done there, I want to share something with you?" Without waiting for a reply, He turned and walked off toward the chapel.

Oddly enough, during the vision the question never popped into my head, "Well, why did we not just use a bulldozer in the first place?" That thought came later as I reflected about this part of the vision again. Instead, I moved on and did as He said. It was hard work lopping off the vines. They were everywhere and clung to the siding of the chapel with a death grip. It was one thing to cut them, but another thing all together to pull the matted greenery away from the wood and bricks. The work took several hours.

Once I was satisfied all the vines were gone, I put down the loppers and walked up the front steps. Jesus opened the door, and greeted me.   Walking outside, He stood back to see how the chapel looked without all the overgrowth. I asked Him if there was some significance to the vines... "They represent the natural world trying to overtake your faith, and they give a strong indication of a passage of time. When you saw those vines and how hard it was to remove them, did it not illustrate how the natural world had crept in and obscured the spiritual world from your view?"

As we walked back through the doorway, He said "You must be hot and tired! Would you like some ice water?" He motioned to a small folding table near the center of the room. There was a pitcher of ice water sitting on it, along with a couple drinking glasses. "Yes, that would be wonderful!" I said. At that, He walked over to the table and poured me a glass. By the way He watched me drinking it, I perceived there was something special about the water. "This water is significant, isn't it?" I asked.

"Isn't everything?" He remarked. Smiling, He said, "It's Living Water. Do you understand what Living Water is?" I thought I did, so I said, "It's the kind of water that flows up from inside me from the Holy Spirit. Because it flows up from within me, I never thirst for lack of what is needful. It seems to me that it is a metaphor to represent the Kingdom of Heaven manifest in me. This is, because your power flows through me. It is water that provides for all my needs, so much so that I never thirst for what I need." "YES! That's right," He said.

I wondered out loud, "So, is this what you wanted to share with me?" Looking up at the distressed rafters of the building where sunlight was pouring through the holes in the roof, He mumbled, "Well, that's one thing." Then, stretching His arms wide, He spun around in a circle. The light that poured in from the big hole in the roof cast itself upon Him like a spot light. "Have you wondered yet, why this room is empty?" He asked. "There are only these enclaves lining the walls. There are no pews, no pulpit, no other furniture..." I had no clue... so He went on.

"I have called you to fill this place with people, to bring them into the Kingdom of Heaven, and tell them My Good News. I trust you understand I'm not talking about this particular building. You will serve many more than this mere building can seat!" His words caused me to recall reading about Elijah, when the Lord had told him not to despair. He told Elijah He had reserved unto Himself seven thousand men who had not bent their knee to unbelief (any other god).

This passage spoke to me and encouraged me. At the time, this distinct feeling came over me, in the spirit, telling me He was trying to say something important. He was telling me there were thousands of men and women set apart for us to mentor, train, and equip for the Kingdom... These were to be Mighty Men and Powerful Women, set apart for the Kingdom of Heaven and ultimately the presentation of His Bride. "When you understand these things," Jesus went on, "you will understand why I have called you the Repairer of the Breach."

Abruptly, He turned and said, "Now, come with Me, and we'll give you what you asked for!" He motioned me to follow Him to the corner cabinet, that He had pointed to a couple nights before. Once again, a brilliant white light poured out into the room as He opened the door. Reaching inside, He retrieved a small ball of white light about the size of a soft ball.

"Kneel down," He told me. Having done as instructed, He then laid the ball of light upon my head. The warmth of it felt nice. Then, it just seemed to melt away. In its place, was the sensation of wholeness and healing! I was very grateful to receive it!" At that moment, I fully expected to NEVER be attacked by intense headaches again.

As He helped me to my feet, He looked into my eyes intently and asked, "Ryker, will you feed My sheep?" Meeting His gaze, I replied "Yes, Lord!" Again, He asked, "Ryker, will you feed My lambs?" "Of course I will," I responded. Once more, He asked, "Ryker, will you feed My sheep?" Whereupon I responded for the third time, "You know I will, Lord..." Then the vision ended.

Upon opening my eyes, I remembered the Lord had asked me to walk out under the stars to the North Gate. So, gathering up my sword and shield, which I had brought up the sandy hill with me, I went over to the gate. Once there, the Lord told me to declare to the spiritual world what I had received these past few nights; and take ownership of what had been given to me. So, I spoke out loud the blessings that were now mine, and the glory that is to come.

PERSONAL COMMENTARY

This was a fairly long and considerably more elaborate vision. A number of things stand out as meaningful:

The original road bed:

Up until this point, it never occurred to me that it was odd that there wasn't any access to this little chapel in the woods. We all know how dreams and visions often seem to defy logic. So we easily dismiss and overlook the unrealistic. Discovering the original road bed therefore deepened the plot. It told me there had been a road once. It must have been traveled upon for many years (in the first century church). It spoke of life in the past. As we discussed already, the path represents the truth which had long since been over grown by the advance of nature (the natural world). Finding this developed road reminded me of a Scripture (a Rhema word to me-i.e. personal word from the Bible) God gave me back in 1995…

"And those from <u>among you</u> will <u>rebuild the ancient ruins</u>; You <u>will raise up the age-old foundations</u>; And you will be called the <u>Repairer of the Breach, The Restorer of the streets</u> in which to dwell."   Isaiah 58:12 (NASB)

At that time, we were directionless and drifting like a sailing ship on a glassy sea. We longed to hear something about our future. During a prayer meeting at church, the Lord answered our question. One of the things He said to me was "Isaiah 58:12." This verse was to become a significant guiding beacon that led us toward our destiny.

This passage was followed up, a number of years later, by another:

"Since thou wast precious in my sight, thou hast been honorable, and I have loved thee: therefore will I give men for thee, and people for thy life. Fear not: for I am with thee: I will bring thy seed from the east, and gather thee from the west; I will say to the north, Give up; and to the south, Keep not back: bring my sons from far and my daughters from the ends of the earth; Even everyone that is called by my name: for I have created him for my glory, I have formed him; yea, I have made him."   Isaiah 43:4-7 (KJV)

And another:

"Enlarge the place of thy tent, and let them stretch forth the curtains of thine habitations: spare not, lengthen thy cords, and strengthen thy stakes; For thou shalt break forth on the right hand and on the left; and thy seed shall inherit the Gentiles, and <u>make the desolate cities to be inhabited</u>."

Isaiah 54:2-3 (KJV)

In each of these passages, He speaks of a great gathering of mighty men and powerful women for the restoration of what once was. These passages are not only for me, but for those who persevere to do His will. For we are about to see the restoration of the Kingdom of Heaven upon the earth. God's will shall be done upon the earth as it is in Heaven, and as it was in Adam's day before his disobedience.

"For the anxious longing of the creation waits eagerly for <u>the revealing of the sons of God</u>. For the creation was subjected to futility, not of its own will, but because of Him who subjected it, in hope that the creation itself also will be set free from its slavery to corruption in <u>the freedom of the glory of the children of God</u>. For we know that the whole creation groans and suffers the pains of childbirth together until now. And not only this, but also we ourselves, having the first fruits of the Spirit, <u>even we ourselves groan within ourselves</u>, <u>waiting eagerly for our adoption as sons, the redemption of our body</u>." **Romans 8:19-23 (NASB)**

"After this manner therefore pray ye: Our Father which art in Heaven, Hallowed be thy name. <u>Thy Kingdom Come. Thy Will be Done in Earth, as it is in Heaven</u>...." **Matthew 6:9-10 (KJV)**

"God standeth in the <u>Congregation of the Mighty</u> (this is referring to us -the sons of God or more specifically the children of the Most High)**; He judgeth among the gods** (you will see in a minute that He is referring to us as gods, that is lower case "g" gods as in children of God)**. How long will ye** (the children of the Most High) **judge unjustly, and accept the persons of the wicked? Selah.** (Here He is asking these questions of us, and He then instructs as following:) **Defend the poor and fatherless: do justice to the afflicted and needy. Deliver the poor and needy: rid them out of the hand of the wicked. They** (the poor and needy) **know not, neither will they understand; they walk on in darkness:**

all the foundations of the earth are out of course. (Here He refers again to the same thing he said about creation being subjected to futility by the fall of man in Romans 8:19-23, again indicating that this is not the way it is meant to be under our reign – The Earth is out of sorts or in contradiction to the will of God concerning it) **I have said, Ye are gods; and all of you are children of the most High.** But (because we do not believe God, exercise our authority and responsibilities upon the earth, nor cause His will to be done on Earth as it is in Heaven) **ye shall die like men, and fall like one of the princes** (You shall be subject to the laws of nature and die like men instead of thrive like the way the sons of God / children of the Most High are meant to live on this Earth). **Arise, O God, judge the earth: for thou shalt inherit all nations."** **Psalm 82:1-8 (KJV)**

And finally…**"Now it will come about that in the last days the mountain of the house of the LORD will be established as the chief of the mountains, And will be raised above the hills; And all the nations will stream to it. And many peoples will come and say, 'Come, let us go up to the mountain of the LORD, To the house of the God of Jacob; That He may teach us concerning His ways And that we may walk in His paths.' For the law will go forth from Zion and the word of the LORD from Jerusalem."** **Isaiah 2:2-3 (KJV)**

Then, referring to Adam' s destruction and Christ's restoration.

"For if by one man's offence (Adam) **death reigned by one; MUCH MORE they which receive abundance of grace and of the gift of righteousness shall REIGN in LIFE by one, Jesus Christ…For as by one man's disobedience many were made sinners, so by the obedience of One** (Jesus) **shall many be made righteous. Moreover the law entered, that the offence might abound. But where sin abounded, grace did MUCH MORE abound: That as sin hath reigned unto death, even so might grace reign through righteousness unto eternal life by Jesus Christ our Lord."** **Romans 5:17 (KJV)**

Cup of Cold Water:

Regarding the living water: The concept of Living Water is crucial to understanding the reality of the Secret Place. The secret place that Psalm 91:1 alludes to ("He that dwelleth in the secret place of the Most High, shall abide under the Shadow of the

Almighty") is the place where God's Spirit dwells. That place is within us. It is in and through our spirit that His Spirit both dwells and flows.

"Jesus answered and said unto her, 'If thou knewest the gift of God, and Who it is that saith to thee, Give me to drink; thou wouldest have asked of Him, and He would have given thee living water.' The woman saith unto Him, 'Sir, thou hast nothing to draw with, and the well is deep: from whence then hast thou that living water? Art Thou greater than our father Jacob, which gave us the well, and drank thereof himself, and his children, and his cattle?' Jesus answered and said unto her, 'Whosoever drinketh of this water shall thirst again: But whosoever drinketh of the water that I shall give him shall never thirst; but the water that I shall give him shall be in him a well of water springing up into everlasting life.' The woman saith unto Him, 'Sir, give me this water, that I thirst not, neither come hither to draw."

John 4:10-15 (KJV)

In this way, the Holy Spirit manifests Himself as an artesian well. Now, rather than us going to the well, the well actually springs up from within us. It overflows our ability to contain it, and refreshes all who come near.   To walk in the Spirit, means to dwell in the Spirit. It means we live in a place where there is no doubt, nor unbelief regarding the power of the Word of God. We relinquish ourselves to be a river of blessing to the world, in whatever manner God wishes to use us.   In this way, this secret place is not somewhere to go, rather it is carried within us as much as our own heart. We never thirst again, for we are constantly supplied with fresh living water, as the Holy Spirit gushes up from within.

"The Kingdom of God cometh not with observation: Neither shall they say 'Lo here! Or, Lo there!' For, behold the Kingdom of God is within you."

Luke 17:20-21 (KJV)

The empty chapel:

In the empty chapel, He takes this opportunity to speak of the future. His intent is to declare that the ancient ruins must be rebuilt. And that it is now the anointed time to call and equip mighty men and powerful women for the "revealing of the Sons of God." This may not be so obvious from the content of this vision alone. Additional content from subsequent visions will eventually merge into this scene.

"For the anxious longing of the creation waits eagerly for The Revealing of the Sons of God. For (because) **the creation was subjected to futility, not of its own will, but because of Him who subjected it, in hope that the creation itself also will be set free from its slavery to corruption in the freedom of the glory of the children of God.** For we know that **the whole creation groans and suffers the pains of childbirth together until NOW.** And not only this, but also we ourselves, having **the first fruits of the Spirit, even we ourselves groan within ourselves, waiting eagerly for our adoption as sons, the redemption of our body."**   **Romans 8:19-23 (NASB)**

One of those Scriptures He shared with me refers to seven thousand men whom He has reserved for Himself.

But what saith the answer of God unto him? I have reserved to myself seven thousand men, who have not bowed the knee to *the image of* **Baal. In the same way then, there has also come to be at the present time a remnant according to God's gracious choice....**   **Romans 11:4-5 (KJV)**

He has spoken to me that He will choose the same number out of this generation. He spoke of how He has already sanctified them (set them aside) for the spiritual conquest of the earth. For this earth is about to be won back from the hands of the devil. Again, this is for another book. But it is important to mention in order to lend understanding to the vision, as it unfolds.

After the healing, He also took the opportunity to repeat the same three questions He had asked Peter. Even during the moment, I understood what was going on. He was driving home that there is a reason for all the blessings He is offering here in this secret place. And here is His reason: "People are the whole point."

"But this I say, 'He which soweth sparingly shall reap also sparingly; and he which soweth bountifully shall reap also bountifully. Every man according as he purposeth in his heart, so let him give; not grudgingly, or of necessity: for God loveth a cheerful giver.' And God is able to make all grace abound toward you; that ye, always having all sufficiency in all things, may abound to every good work: (As it is written, He hath dispersed abroad; he hath given to the poor: his righteousness remaineth forever. Now he that ministereth seed to the sower both ministers bread for your food, and multiplies your seed sown, and increases the fruits of your righteousness;) Being enriched in everything to all bountifulness, which causeth through us

thanksgiving to God. <u>For the administration of this service not only supplieth the want of the saints, but is abundant also by many thanksgivings unto God;"</u>   **2 Corinthians 9:6-12 (KJV)**

He blesses us, so that we can be a blessing. His blessings are not meant to be used to build bigger barns for ourselves. We were never meant to be reservoirs for God's blessings. We are meant to be rivers, through which His blessings flow to the world. To me, He was saying, "Ryker, do you understand how important this is to me? Do you understand that I am depending upon you? Do you understand that I am trusting you with the future?" It was both humbling and glorious to consider the mere notion that the Creator of the Universe was choosing to trust me. What an inconceivable concept. Trusting Him was all I had ever known. But, Him trusting us? Nevertheless, is that not what He was asking Peter? "Can I trust you to do what I have called you to do?" Peter's response? "Lord, You know all things, therefore You must know that I will."

Declaring the Word:

The last thing worthy of mention, are the instructions to go declare these things He gave me. In my experience, every time He gives me something in the Spirit (which He intends to manifest in the natural world), He instructs me to receive it by speaking the words audibly. This understanding was common to me even at the time of this vision. Spiritual faith begins in our heart, but does not manifest itself in the natural world until we speak it. That is how God created the world, that is how we receive our eternal salvation, and is also how we receive our physical healings and other answers to prayer in the natural world. Words are spiritual vessels which hold our authority and power, for both saved and unsaved people. But the Word of God spoken by a believer always has prevailing authority.

"That if thou shalt confess <u>with thy mouth</u> the Lord Jesus, and shalt believe in thine heart that God hath raised Him from the dead, thou shalt be saved. <u>For with the heart man believeth unto righteousness; and with the mouth confession</u> is made unto salvation."   **Romans 10:9-10 (KJV)**

You may have taken note of the sword and shield being mentioned. There is an unmistakable truth about God, which is evident in His word. He loves metaphors, parables, and symbols. In this way, He has given me a few items to implement into my spiritual warfare time. Two of those items are a sword and shield. Like no other symbols could, they represent the Word of God, Faith, and the conquest of our adversary's kingdom.

"For the Word of God is quick and powerful, and sharper than any two edged sword, piercing even to the dividing asunder of soul and spirit, and of the joints and marrow, and is a discerner of the thoughts and intents of the heart." Hebrews 4:12 (KJV)

"Above all taking the shield of faith, wherewith ye shall be able to quench all the fiery darts of the wicked. And take the helmet of salvation, and the Sword of the Spirit, which is the Word of God." Ephesians 6:16-17 (KJV)

The North Gate:

"The North Gate" is an actual gate to a corral situated between our home and the Marine base where we serve. It is my primary place to meet the Lord at night. This particular gate is meaningful to me, because it was a point of beginning for what has become North Gate Ministries.

It all really began one night in Montana back in 2008. When we met that night, He said "Follow me, I have something I would like to show you that you started." It was dark outside, but I did not hesitate to follow. We walked down our driveway, which wanders through the woods, until we came to our log gate entrance. Once there, He told me to stop. I asked Him what He wanted to show me. I was not certain how He could show me anything, as dark as it was outside.

He said, "close your eyes." I had no idea how closing my eyes was going to help me see better, but I complied. Then He said, "tell me what you hear." I listened for a moment, but it was a very peaceful night. I said, "I don't hear anything Lord." He only responded more emphatically. "Listen, and tell me what you hear." I listened more intently for any sound at all. Then I said, "I do hear the river running on the other side of the highway." "That's right," He said, "...and so I have made you into a river, and I am sending you to a dry and thirsty land. There you will flow."

Where did He send us? He sent us to the Mojave Desert, in Southern California. I still remember the day we left. I was hiking up the mountain, to disconnect the water line from our spring box. As I pulled my way through the brush, the Lord called my name. I stopped, and said, "Yes Lord." "Ryker," He said, "I just want you to know where you are going, I am sending you." I burst out in tears. Never before had I been given the assured knowledge (that only a word from the Lord can give a person) that God was sending me to the place I was going. I had supposed (and trusted) He was with me wherever I went. But never before had I embarked out into the unknown, with the confidence that can only come from hearing His voice on the matter. With everything we had been through in the past, and the unknown that lay before us again, it was wonderful to know everything was going to be just fine. About a week before this statement, God had been assuring us in other ways about the blessings that were approaching us. On a prayer walk around our property one day, my wife, Belle, asked if she and our young daughters could join me. It seemed that it would be good, for our daughters, to see what Daddy does with the Lord, so I agreed.

On our way to one of the property markers, Belle was reading a passage I had selected. In the passage God was promising His rain (blessings). Suddenly, it started raining on us. We thought this was a cool coincidence, and remarked to each other about it. When we looked up in the sky though, we noted there was not a single cloud to be seen. That's when our wonder began to rise. We further noted it was ONLY raining on us. Around us was a wet circle about sixteen feet wide. Whoa!!! We knew, for sure, this was no longer a coincidence. We rejoiced in the rain for a few moments, and thanked God for the miracle. However, He was not done yet. When we started off toward home, amazingly the circle of rain actually followed us for a few minutes before finally subsiding. And true to form, His rain (blessings) followed us to the desert, and have been with us ever since.

On our way to the desert, I asked Him where we would live when we got here. When we left, we had packed up everything into a U-Haul and took off without knowing anything more than the town we were going to. He said, "Don't worry about it, you will know it when you see it." I said, "All I really ask is for us to live as close to the U.S. Marine Base as possible. This will make it much easier to serve the young Marines much more effectively.

When we got to our destination, He provided us a temporary home for expediency sake; but I knew it was not our home. We stayed there for several months, while we continued to look for our home. Then, one day I heard about the house we live in now. The next morning I left for work early and stopped by this place. Walking in the back door, I went straight through the living room and out the sliding glass front door. There, in front of me, was the Marine base. It turned out this was the very closest house to the main gate of the Marine Base. It was instantly clear to me that this was our home.

At the time, the house was in the middle of renovation and would not be ready for a few weeks. We knew it was ours though, so we were willing to be patient. Every day I would leave for work early, so I could take some time to walk around the house to pray. I wanted to spiritually prepare this home to house my family. First off, I started looking for a place to meet the Lord. Out in front of the house was a horse corral with a big beam gate. When standing on our patio, we can actually look through the gate to see the Marine Base. I decided this was where the Lord and I would meet, and asked Him if this was acceptable. He agreed. Turning around to face our house, I raised my hands and began to pray over it.

The Lord interrupted me, and asked me to stop for a moment. I stopped, and He said, "Turn around." I did so, and found myself facing the military base. Then He said, "Now pray in that direction." I smiled with understanding, and began to pray over the base. When I was done, the Lord said "Ryker, you are going to start a ministry here and you will call it "The North Gate." I repeated the words several times, and told Him I really liked the sound of that. It was so exciting that I called my wife immediately to tell her what God had said.

When I shared this new revelation with her, though, she was quiet for moment. Then she said, "When you get home tonight, I have to show you something from what God told me to read this morning." When I got home from work, she excitedly told me to sit down as she got her Bible. While she was out of the room, God said "Ryker, listen to your wife. What she is going to read is for you." A moment later she returned. Flipping through her Bible, she found Ezekiel 47 and began to read.

"Afterward he (The angel of the Lord) **brought me again <u>unto the door of the house; and, behold, waters issued out from under the threshold of the house eastward</u>: for the forefront of the house stood toward the east, and the waters came down from under from the right side of the house, at the south side of the altar. Then <u>brought he me out of the way of the gate northward</u>** ("The North Gate" in NASB)**, and led me about the way without unto the utter** (Outer) **gate by the way that looketh eastward; and, behold, there ran out waters on the right side.**

And when the man that had the line in his hand went forth eastward, <u>he measured a thousand cubits</u>, and he brought me through the waters; the

waters were to the ankles. Again he measured a thousand, and brought me through the waters; the waters were to the knees. Again he measured a thousand, and brought me through; the waters were to the loins. <u>Afterward he measured a thousand; and it was a river that I could not pass over: for the waters were risen, waters to swim in, a river that could not be passed over</u>. And he said unto me, 'Son of man, hast thou seen this?' Then he brought me, and caused me to return to the brink of the river.

Now when I had returned, behold, at the bank of the river were very many trees on the one side and on the other. Then said he unto me, '<u>These waters issue out toward the east country, and go down into the desert</u>, and go into the sea: which being brought forth into the sea, the waters shall be healed. <u>And it shall come to pass, that everything that liveth, which moveth, whithersoever the rivers shall come, shall live</u>: and there shall be a very great multitude of fish, because these waters shall come thither: <u>for they shall be healed; and everything shall live whither the river cometh</u>.

And it shall come to pass, that the fishers shall stand upon it from En-gedi even unto En-eglaim; they shall be a place to spread forth nets; their fish shall be according to their kinds, as the fish of the great sea, exceeding many. <u>But the miry places thereof and the marshes thereof shall not be healed; they shall be given to salt</u>. And by the river upon the bank thereof, on this side and on that side, <u>shall grow all trees for meat, whose leaf shall not fade, neither shall the fruit thereof be consumed: it shall bring forth new fruit according to his months, because their waters they issued out of the sanctuary: and the fruit thereof shall be for meat, and the leaf thereof for medicine</u>." **Ezekiel 47:1-12 (ESV)**

From this, The North Gate came to be. Along with it, came the blessings and prophesies of Ezekiel associated with it as well. Before departing this conversation though, it would be enjoyable to share two amusing stories which deeply blessed us. The underlined parts of the Scriptures above are highlighted to illustrate how these stories were used to reflect God's humor and the affirmation of His word to us:

"Behold, Waters issued out from under the Threshold of the House:" (vs. 1)

Shortly before moving into the house, we stopped to see how the renovations were coming. Belle went to the bedrooms to check out the fresh paint. I went to the kitchen to see if the cabinets were installed yet. They were not. Apparently though, one of the workers had left the valve for the new sink open. Water was shooting into the kitchen area. By this time it had flooded the entire kitchen <u>and was now pouring through the open door out over the threshold</u>. Outside it had formed a stream, and was flowing over the patio. My jaw dropped in amazement as I suddenly became aware of the spiritual significance of this scene. I called Belle in. The moment she walked in the room and saw what I was looking at, we both began to laugh. How cool was this? We stood and watched it for a moment, then reluctantly turned the valve off.

"The Man (Angel of the Lord) that had the line in His hand went forth eastward, He measured a Thousand Cubits." (vs. 3)

The next story occurred after we had settled into our new home. In the middle of one night, the Lord woke me and said, "Ryker, let's go for a walk." Still being a little groggy, I said, "Lord, can it wait? I'm really tired." He replied, "Come on, it will be fun!" Not wanting to quench the Spirit, (especially as enthusiastic as He was about this walk), I asked Him to give me a moment to find my slippers. After putting my slippers on, I walked outside and asked where He wanted to go. He simply said, "straight ahead." So, off we went. On our walk, we had a leisurely conversation about things on both our minds. It was actually quite enjoyable, despite it being so early in the morning. The moon was full and bright. Its light made seeing our way through the desert terrain very easy.

He was right, the walk was fun. It did not occur to me to ask if we were going anywhere in particular. Soon, it became evident though that we were heading directly toward the Marine Base fence. Despite this realization, I never said anything about it. It seemed safe to assume it was His intent for me to pray over the base. We had been doing that a great deal lately. We just kept walking and talking though. When we finally arrived at the fence, He simply quit talking. Assuming this was my cue, I took the fence in both hands and began to pray. After having finished, I turned and started to step off toward home. My thinking was that we would resume our conversation during the return trip.

However, He said, "Count your steps." Confused, I asked, "Why?" He just repeated Himself, "Count your steps." "But Lord," I said, "you know I can't walk and chew bubble gum at the same time," (referring to my intent to continue our previous conversation). He merely repeated Himself once more. "Fine," I said, "Let's count my steps." So off we went, with me wondering what the point of this little exercise was. It seemed meaningless, and was even a little irritating, until I got about 700 paces into it.

Looking at where I stood, in relationship to the fence in front of our house, something suddenly occurred to me. "I know how this count is going to end," I remarked, "it will be exactly 1,000 paces from the Marine Base fence to our fence." With this thought in mind, I hurried on, intrigued. Sure enough, a few moments later I counted "999" Then taking one more step, I reached out with my hand, took ahold of the fence, and counted "1,000!"

Excitedly running into the house, I woke Belle and told her what had just happened. We laughed and rejoiced together at 3 a.m., about all the implications regarding His word over the newly formed North Gate Ministries. We also contemplated about all the planning (on God's part), that it must have taken to make sure our fence was exactly 1,000 of "my size paces" from the Marine Base fence. All this, just to be reminded of what the Angel of the Lord had also measured out for Ezekiel. There have certainly been numerous monumental events to reveal His purposes, but nothing seems to impact us so deeply as the good humor of our Lord.

Bull Dozer:

It seems like bringing in the bulldozer to begin with would have made so much more sense. Nevertheless, it is easy to imagine why He had me clear the path by hand. People are complex. They don't do well with bulldozing their whole set of values and ideals. I was no different. He did not attempt to reveal, or explain, or instruct me in these matters of the Spirit all at once. Had He done so, it's quite certain, I would have rejected and / or at the least resisted it bitterly.

He simply started by getting a wedge of Truth in. Then He made sure it sunk a little further. Admittedly though, there came a time when I had my interest piqued enough to pass the "point of no return." By then, I was ready to throw everything to the test and see what would be left of it afterwards. During that intense, Spirit-led learning time, the Lord utilized the ministry efforts of others. Like a bulldozer behind schedule, God used sermons, conferences, books, CD's, and voluminous other resources to plow through my world.

The Vines:

We have already made reference to the metaphorical value of the vines. Unbelief, and familiarity with the natural world and what to expect from it, had rooted deeply and taken over my life. It was impossible to get my prayers answered, and live anything remotely close to the victorious life God intended, because it just wasn't considered "normal." All of the unbelief was the result of past unanswered prayers, and my expectations associated with them. During this time, I was cutting and pulling away at this doubt, unbelief, and negative self-talk with the powerful Word of Truth. I was also armed with a new-found decision to believe everything God said, irregardless of the past. I did so by taking responsibility for my past faithlessness, and repenting of it.

LIVING WATER

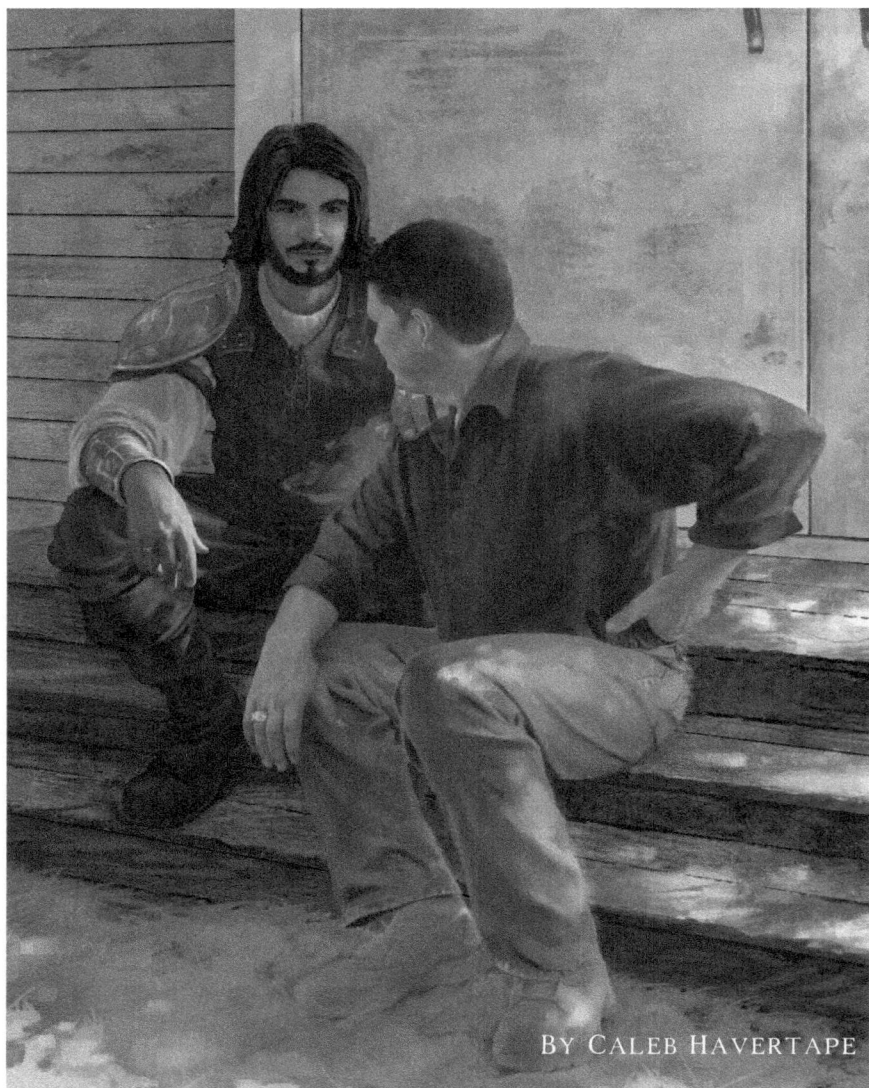

BY CALEB HAVERTAPE

Chapter Five

A New Backbone

Since the first visions involving healing of chronic acid reflux and severe headaches, there has been no further trouble with them. That is not to say they did not threaten to return, as all temptations do. However they were dealt with in faith, as all temptations must be. Usually when a temptation comes and attempts to own me, my response is: "I don't THINK so!" It is crucial to verbally remind our body (and demonic forces) that despite every temptation to believe otherwise, these healings are a past event.

Being healed is the easy part. Staying healed, on the other hand, is difficult. Virtually any Christian can experience a random leap of faith which may result in a healing. To walk in faith every day and maintain God's gifts though, takes an intensely persistent bull-dog kind of faith. We absolutely MUST choose not to look at the outward appearance of things. Rather, focus earnestly on the Word of God regarding the matter.

There are two realities which we may choose to submit to. There are no alternatives other than these. As long as we live and breathe, we will be in submission to one of them. They are what we see, or what we know. Walking in the Spirit is not natural; it is a choice. And it always flies in the face of what our senses and our brain tell us. At those times, it cannot be overemphasized how important it is to declare audibly, "It is written: by His stripes we are healed, in Jesus' name..." When pressing through and binding the repeated temptations (symptoms) in the past, they always went away. After a few victories in this manner, rarely are they ever seen again. In our minds, there are often many strongholds of unbelief. Consequently, some healings and deliverances are bound to be more difficult and protracted than others.

When those strongholds are identified, they have to be dealt with. We must lay siege to them and cut them off from the resources that supply them, i.e. lies....and more often than not...fear itself. Then we must saturate the lies with 'faith in action'. If we are sick, then go about our business as if we weren't. If we are poor, then we put the little we have to work, so God can increase our abundance.

"Hitherto have ye asked nothing <u>IN MY NAME</u>: <u>ASK, AND YE SHALL RECEIVE</u>, that your joy may be full. These things have I spoken unto you in proverbs: but the time cometh, when <u>I shall no more speak unto you in proverbs</u>, but <u>I shall shew you plainly of the Father</u>. At that day <u>ye shall ask in My name</u>: and I say not unto you, that I will pray the Father for you: For the Father Himself loveth you, because ye have loved Me, and have believed that I came out from God."   **John 16:24-27 (KJV)**

If we ask in His name, we <u>WILL</u> receive. The reason we will receive, is so that His chief concern may be met. As any godly husband desires for his bride, God's goal is to **make our joy complete**. He further points out that He used to purposely speak in vague parables and proverbs. Now, however, He will no longer do so. Instead, He will show us plainly what the Father wants us to know and He expects us to understand. When that happens (when we understand) we will always have what we ask for, because He will pray to the Father for us. We will have it because He loves us, because we loved His Son, and believe that He came from God.

"Wherein He hath abounded toward us in all wisdom and prudence; having made known to unto us the mystery of His Will, according to His good pleasure which He hath purposed in Himself."   **Ephesians 1:8-9 (KJV)**

"It is the Spirit that quickeneth; the flesh profiteth nothing: The words that I speak unto you, <u>they are spirit, and they are life</u>."   **John 6:63 (KJV)**

Here are some important points. Jesus was not able to do miracles because He was God. For in fact, He had subjected himself to the limitations of being a man. The reason He was able to perform miracles was because the Holy Spirit dwelled in and flowed through Him. Remember, He kept telling people that these miracles were proof that He was sent from the Father. It was the Holy Spirit that healed people, not Jesus (at least not independently or directly). And the only reason all this was possible, was because He had **no sin**. He was a suitable dwelling place for the Spirit of the Most High. He was the first living Holy of Holies (dwelling place of God).

It is no different for us. This is how we also perform miracles. The same Holy Spirit dwells in us and flows through us. And, He does so for the same reason. Miracles are only possible for those who are just as sinless as Jesus. That is, only those who possess His righteousness. Without the righteousness of Jesus, the Holy Spirit cannot dwell in us. Without the Holy Spirit, we are powerless to do the supernatural.

It is the Holy Spirit who brings life to our mortal bodies. We can do what we may to preserve our bodies through eating right, exercising, and other means. In the end though, all we have done at best is post-pone our death. Consequently, my chief concern should not be to merely eat well, exercise, and take care of my body. I do those things, as any wise steward should. But, I am not depending upon any of these things to give me health or extend my life. I do my part as a wise steward, but recognize that it is God's Word and His Spirit that gives me life.

"There is therefore now no condemnation to them which are in Christ Jesus, who walk not after the flesh, but after the Spirit. For the law of the Spirit of life in Christ Jesus hath made me free from the law of sin and death. For what the law could not do, in that it was weak through the flesh, God sending his own Son in the likeness of sinful flesh, and for sin, condemned sin in the flesh: That the righteousness of the law might be fulfilled in us, who walk not after the flesh, but after the Spirit. FOR THEY THAT ARE (live) **AFTER THE FLESH DO MIND THE THINGS OF THE FLESH; BUT THEY THAT ARE** (live) **AFTER THE SPIRIT THE THINGS OF THE SPIRIT. For to be carnally minded is death; but to be spiritually minded is life and peace. Because the carnal mind is enmity against God: for it is not subject to the law of God, neither indeed can be. So then they that are in the flesh cannot please God. But ye are not in the flesh, but in the Spirit, if so be that the Spirit of God dwell in you.**

Now if any man have not the Spirit of Christ, he is none of His. And if Christ be in you, the body is dead because of sin; but the Spirit is life because of righteousness. But if the Spirit of Him that raised up Jesus from the dead dwell in you, He that raised up Christ from the dead shall also quicken (give life to) **your mortal bodies by His Spirit that dwelleth in you. Therefore, brethren, WE ARE NOT DEBTORS, NOT TO THE FLESH, TO LIVE AFTER THE FLESH."** Romans 8:1-12 (KJV)

"And Jesus answered him, saying, 'It is written, that man shall not live by bread alone, BUT BY EVERY WORD OF GOD." Luke 4:4 (KJV)

"For BODILY EXERCISE PROFITHETH LITTLE: but godliness is profitable unto ALL things, HAVING PROMISE FOR THIS TIME THAT NOW IS, and of that which is to come." 1 Timothy 4:8 (KJV)

It would also help to read the latter end of Romans chapter seven. It speaks of the sin that dwells in our mortal bodies, and of our righteousness in Christ. Paul goes on to say that those who choose to walk in the Spirit are not under condemnation any longer. We are free from the law of the sin and death (the fallen world). The law of righteousness is fulfilled in us (those who walk by the Spirit). As you read on, you will see how the Spirit dwells in and flows through us. You will also read how we are no longer in debt to the flesh, for we live in a completely different reality. We should choose this day where our allegiances lay; with this kingdom (yours) or His Kingdom?

"We have this treasure in earthen vessels, that the excellency of the power may be of God, and not of us. We are troubled on every side, yet not distressed; we are perplexed, but not in despair; Persecuted, but not forsaken; cast down, but not destroyed; Always bearing about in the body the dying of the Lord Jesus, THAT THE LIFE ALSO OF JESUS MIGHT BE MADE MANIFEST IN OUR BODY

For we which live are alway delivered unto death for Jesus' sake, THAT THE LIFE ALSO OF JESUS MIGHT BE MADE MANIFEST IN OUR MORTAL FLESH. So then death worketh in us, but life in you. We having the same spirit of faith, according as it is written, I believed, and therefore have I spoken; we also believe, and therefore speak; Knowing that He which raised up the Lord Jesus shall raise up us also by Jesus, and shall present us with you.

For all things are for your sakes, that the abundant grace might through the thanksgiving of many rebound to the glory of God. For which cause we faint not; but though our outward man perish, yet the inward man is renewed day by day. For our light affliction, which is but for a moment, worketh for us a far more exceeding and eternal weight of glory; WHILE WE LOOK NOT AT THE THINGS WHICH ARE SEEN, BUT AT THE THINGS WHICH ARE NOT SEEN: for the things which are seen are temporal; but the things which are not seen are eternal." 2 Corinthians 4:7-18 (ESV)

Important Note!

__Always bearing about in the body the dying of the Lord Jesus, THAT THE LIFE ALSO OF JESUS MIGHT BE MADE MANIFEST IN OUR BODY__. How many have totally missed the whole point of this scripture, despite how obvious it is? This is not a Scripture that encourages martyrdom. But, in fact, it means the opposite! Things come against us (illness and trouble) SO THAT we can overcome them, and show the world how much more powerful Jesus' completed work is! "By His stripes we are healed." -Isaiah 53:5 That is, we carry within ourselves the answer to every trespassing danger that approaches us! If it helps, think of Him being like an immunization. So, when sickness or other such trespasses arrive at our door (our body) His suffering (His dying) is there waiting within us to destroy the trespasser. Why does He do this? Read it again...**So, that the life (not death) of Christ might prove itself to be true in our bodies**. What did He purchase with His suffering? Life.

Refusing healing, though the Truth be revealed to you, is not so different than refusing healing from a doctor. Refusing Truth, is like refusing immunizations. Our bodies' ability to resist danger lies dormant, unprepared to meet the threat. If we refuse to receive healing (because of unbelief or ignorance of the Truth), then the truth is not made manifest (our healing does not become real) in us. The price then that He paid on our behalf, is vain and worthless. When I don't get healed, what do I prove other than that the world is right when they say, "God cannot be relied upon?" How can God be blamed for us being weak in faith?

This is what we are doing every time we receive suffering and say, "it must be God's Will." In saying that, we are declaring to the world that God is not a good God, and most certainly not One to be relied upon. But explain to me how God is to be blamed for us not acting upon what He has provided for us. Is it the medical profession's fault if we don't seek their assistance? Or if we do, but don't take the treatment they prescribe?

Read again: "**we look not at the things which are seen, but at the things which are not seen: for the things which are seen are temporal; but the things which are not seen are eternal.**"

Here is another important passage that is so frequently misused by Christians:

There hath no <u>temptation</u> taken you but such as is common to man: but God is faithful, Who will not suffer you to be tempted above what you are able; but will with the temptation also <u>make a way of escape</u>, that ye may be able to bear it."   **1 Corinthians 10:13 (KJV)**

Somehow, people twist this passage to say God will never give you more trouble than you can handle. How they get that from this verse, I am at a loss to know. It's a lie though. It contradicts the rest of God's Word in so many innumerable ways. First and foremost, I promise God will ALWAYS allow more trouble into your life than you can possibly handle. After all, that is the whole point! I mean, He wants you to dwell in the impossible at all times. That is how His strength is perfected in our weakness. If we could handle the trouble ourselves, for what possible reason would we need Him? But again, even this is not what the passage is talking about. It is not talking about trouble, it is about temptation. Temptation is a line of thought which attempts to persuade us to think or do something that is wrong. Has anyone ever been tempted to do the right thing? No, of course not. Granted, trouble can also be a temptation. That is, when trouble comes, and we are tempted to believe in the trouble's ability to do what it threatens to do; rather than believing in what God's Word promises to do.

There are three primary temptations that the tempter releases upon us; the lust of the eyes, the lust of the flesh, and the boastful pride of life. This has never changed since the Garden of Eden. Our tempter is not that creative. Then again, why should he need to be? These temptations work very well. They are highly effective. Let's simplify it even further. All three temptations are rooted in a single temptation, "Unbelief."

1 Corinthians 10:13 says He will not permit a temptation to approach us which He has not already made a way of escape from. That way is "Truth." Think about it.

Let's start with the first time the three temptations were deployed on earth.

Genesis 3:1-6

"Now the serpent was more subtle than any beast of the field which the LORD God had made. And he said unto the woman,"

Serpent: **"Yea, hath God said, Ye shall not eat of every tree of the garden?"**

Eve: **And the woman said unto the serpent, "We may eat of the fruit of the trees of the garden: But of the fruit of the tree which is in the midst of the garden, God hath said, Ye shall not eat of it, neither shall ye touch it, lest ye die."**

Serpent: **And the serpent said unto the woman, "Ye shall not surely die: For God doth know that in the day ye eat thereof, then your eyes shall be opened, and ye shall be as gods, knowing good and evil."**

Eve: **And when the woman saw that the tree was <u>good for food</u>– (Lust of the Fles And that it was <u>pleasant to the eyes</u>– (Lust of the Eyes) And to be <u>desired to make one wise</u>– (Pride of Life) She took of the fruit thereof, and did eat" (KJV)**

Attempting to hold God to a promise He did not actually make never goes well. Do you see how 1 Cor.10:13 has been misused? So, in reality, what we are actually attempting to do is to hold God to our **understanding** of a promise. Look around, God is giving plenty of Christians more than they can handle. Is He then a liar? No, because despite what someone may have told you, God never actually promised not to give you more trouble than you can handle. He said, He would provide a way out of temptation. Now that, we can count on Him for.

If God's Word says something, then we are duty bound to believe it and receive it (act on it), or suffer the consequences of our unbelief. Always remember it is God's Word that has power, not our words about His. So many people get mad at God for not keeping a promise they themselves put in His mouth. God did not promise more trouble than we can handle. He promised more power to deal with the trouble, no matter how big it is. He promised He would always make a way for us, no matter what temptation presents itself.

So did God make a way for the first woman to be victorious over these temptations of unbelief? Absolutely, Eve knew what God said, all she had to do was repeat it, and stand upon it. Here is how to handle a lie, crush it with the truth. Let's look at someone who handled the same temptations in the right way:

Matthew 4:1-10

Then was Jesus led up of the Spirit into the wilderness to be tempted of the devil.

(The Holy Spirit led Him into the Wilderness….to be tempted.)

And when He had fasted forty days and forty nights, He was afterward an hungered. And when the tempter came to Him, He said,

(Temptation: Lust of the Flesh)

Serpent: "If thou be the Son of God, command that these stones be made bread."
(Jesus' Response: It is Written…)

Jesus: But He answered and said, "IT IS WRITTEN, Man shall not live by bread alone, but by every word that proceedeth out of the mouth of God."

(Temptation: Boastful Pride of Live)

Serpent: Then the devil taketh Him up into the holy city, and setteth Him on a pinnacle of the temple, And saith unto Him, "If thou be the Son of God, cast Thyself down: FOR IT IS WRITTEN, He shall give His angels charge concerning Thee: and in their hands they shall bear Thee up, lest at any time Thou dash Thy foot against a stone."

(Jesus Response: It is Written…)

Jesus: Jesus said unto Him, "IT IS WRITTEN AGAIN, Thou shalt not tempt the Lord thy God."

(Temptation: Lust of the Eyes)

Serpent: Again, the devil taketh Him up into an exceeding high mountain, and sheweth Him all the kingdoms of the world, and the glory of them; And saith unto Him, "All these things will I give Thee, if Thou wilt fall down and worship me."

(Jesus Response: It is Written…)

Then saith Jesus unto him, "Get thee hence, satan: FOR IT IS WRITTEN, Thou shalt worship the Lord thy God, and Him only shalt thou serve." (KJV)

And so should it be with us. There is an escape to every temptation and the answer always begins with: "It is written…"

"He was wounded for our transgressions, He was bruised for our iniquities: the chastisement of our peace was upon Him; and with His stripes we are healed." **Isaiah 53:5 (KJV)**

After so many years of personal suffering and unanswered prayers, it used to be difficult to imagine a person being healed so easily. One of the greatest revelations of our lives, was when we finally realized we were not put on this earth to learn to cope with suffering; but to conquer it.

Now for the vision I had:

After the new-found freedom from these persistent gastric troubles and chronic headaches, the enemy maneuvered in from a new direction. Almost immediately, within days of the relief in those areas, I began to experience a new stiffness in my back. At first it was not so bad. And, I was just too busy with work and ministry matters to deal with it spiritually. Coping with it seemed easier than fighting it with concentrated effort. What a huge mistake! It is costly to learn the hard way. Never give the devil even an inch. Count on it, he WILL take a mile. By the third day of increasing pain, I had to leave work early. The pain had grown so intense I could hardly breathe, much less move around.

Arriving at home, all that could be done was for me to ease into bed and try to sleep it off. Belle said I groaned in pain every time I moved. In the middle of the night though, some wisdom finally overtook me. I asked the Lord if we could meet for healing, then drifted off to sleep once again. Almost immediately, I began to dream. Opening my eyes, I found myself standing on the bottom step of the chapel. Jesus was sitting on the top step motioning for me to join Him. Slowly and painfully, I sat down beside Him. Oddly enough, even in the dream the pain was intense.

"Lord, I don't really feel like working on the chapel today," I said. "I'm in a lot pain. Could I just get a new back first?" "Sure, no problem," He answered, as He briskly stood up and hurried in the front door. Standing up stiffly, I followed Him inside toward the left front corner. We approached an enclave which stood about two places back from the front one. By the time I caught up with Him, He already had its door open.

Light spilled into the room as He put His left hand in and grabbed something long and shiny off a hanger. He turned and held it in front of me, at eye level. "Lie face down," He told me. Once I had done as He instructed, He held it horizontally, and laid it on my back. Whereupon, the light which shone from my "new backbone" dimmed and went out; appearing to have dissolved into me.

Suddenly, the dream ended and I woke up abruptly. Looking over at the clock, I could see it was exactly a half hour after the vision had begun. What a difference that half hour made! After waking from the dream, I purposely tried turning and twisting my back. There was absolutely no pain! It felt so good, I rolled over and kissed My Belle awake. When she woke, I told her all about it... She too, noticed the difference immediately. By then, it was time to get up and go to work. It felt wonderful to zip through the morning and take off for work good as new! It was absolutely amazing. Since then? Not another back problem. How awesome is that?

PERSONAL COMMENTARY

New Back Bone

I don't want to over-spiritualize everything; but it was too irresistible for me not to title this chapter, "A New Backbone." The double meaning is significant, after all that I had gone through to increase in the mental processes necessary to receive this healing. Victory over my own personal circumstances is a process as unique to me, as anyone else's process is to their particular life. Everyone has issues, and rarely are they the same. This much is universal though, the necessity of moving into victory in every aspect of life, most certainly requires "A New Backbone."

Healing itself is a very simple process. Finding faith for it to occur, particularly when one has been around awhile, is very difficult. The saying "You can't teach an old dog new tricks," comes to mind. There is plenty of proof that this saying is not entirely true. For the most part, though, it normally is. Without faith, people are entirely subject to the laws of the natural world. The only exception is, if the influence of someone else's faith is strong enough to overcome our circumstances and unbelief for us.

"If the Spirit of Him that raised up Jesus from the dead dwell in you, <u>He that raised up Christ from the dead shall also quicken your mortal bodies by His Spirit that dwelleth in you</u>. Therefore, brethren, <u>we are debtors, not to the flesh, to live after the flesh</u>." Romans 8:11-12 (KJV)

<u>"Is any among you afflicted?</u> Let him pray. Is any merry? Sing psalms. <u>Is any sick among you? Let him call for the elders of the church; and let them pray over him, anointing him with oil in the name of the Lord: And the prayer of faith shall save the sick, and the Lord shall raise him up</u>; and if he have committed sins, they shall be forgiven him. Confess your faults one to another, and <u>pray one for another, that ye may be healed. The effectual fervent prayer of a righteous man availeth much. Elias was a man subject to like passions as we are</u>, and he prayed earnestly that it might not rain: and it rained not on the earth by the space of three years and six months. And he prayed again, and the Heaven gave rain, and the earth brought forth her fruit." James 5:13-17 (KJV)

Many Christians may experience bursts of faith that produce results. However, to walk in faith daily is exceptionally rare. Having come a long ways in faith myself is gratifying to me. It remains humbling for me, though, when considering how much further there is to go. <u>Faith takes great effort</u>. Despite how true this statement is though, it is not entirely true. It would be more appropriate to say, "the <u>process of growing in faith</u> takes great effort." Faith itself though, is effortless.

To have the faith to declare something is true, while it remains still unseen in the natural world, takes guts. Let me make a bold statement coupled with a challenge. While not intending to minimize the importance of petitionary prayer, I will say this: Of all the miracles, in the Gospels, the Acts, and the letters, <u>nowhere do I see any of them manifest as a result of someone petitioning God in prayer for them</u>.

In every miracle in the New Testament, there is a simple declaration from the one through whom the Holy Spirit flows. Sometimes, there is no prayer or statement at all, such as with the woman who was healed by touching the hem of Jesus' clothes, or with the people who were healed when the disciples shadow touched them. In every instance the healer, whether Jesus or one of His disciples, simply said what must be, as one who has the authority to say so. Recall Jesus' words about the Centurion. He marveled over him, because he understood the power of authority and the spoken word.

"And when Jesus was entered into Capernaum, there came unto Him a centurion, beseeching Him, And saying, 'Lord, my servant lieth at home sick of the palsy, grievously tormented.' And Jesus saith unto him, 'I will come and heal him.' The centurion answered and said, 'Lord, I am not worthy that thou shouldest come under my roof: but <u>speak the word only, and my servant shall be healed. For I am a man under authority, having soldiers under me: and I say to this man, Go, and he goeth; and to another, Come, and he cometh; and to my servant, Do this, and he doeth it</u>.' When Jesus heard it, HE MARVELLED, and said to them that followed, 'Verily I say unto you, <u>I have not found so great faith</u>, no, not in Israel. And I say unto you, That <u>many shall come from the east and west, and shall sit down with Abraham, and Isaac, and Jacob, in the Kingdom of Heaven</u>. BUT THE CHILDREN OF THE KINGDOM SHALL BE CAST OUT INTO OUTER DARKNESS: THERE SHALL BE WEEPING AND GNASHING OF TEETH.' And Jesus said unto the centurion, 'Go thy way; and as thou hast believed, so be it done unto thee.'" And his servant was healed in the selfsame hour. Matt. 8:5-13 (KJV)

Personally, I ceased petitioning for people's healings a long time ago. So often in the past I have heard these words from the Lord, as I began to pray. "Ryker, don't pray it…just say it." Now, I heal people in the omnipotent power of Jesus' Name simply by saying so. "Silver and gold, I may not have, but such as I do have, I give to you…I say, in the Name of Jesus Christ, rise up and walk."

Here is the challenge…. Prove me wrong. Pretend I am from the great state of Missouri, and "show me"! (The Show Me State). Show me where Jesus or the disciples ever petitioned God, in prayer, for someone and they were healed. Remember, petitionary prayer is not wrong, and I am not saying God's word says so. I'm merely saying… that to hope for the best, does not produce the best. Speak as one with authority, because you have been given all authority through the finished work of Christ. Petitionary prayer requires no faith whatsoever; hope maybe, but not faith. There is no faith in hoping something might happen, should the unknowable will of an unknowable god coincide with our request.

With the exception of <u>certain</u> examples in the Old Testament, nowhere do I see petition. I only see declaration. Plainly stated, in regard to the Old Testament; the Kingdom of Heaven had not come yet. It was in fact, still suffering the violence described in Matthew 11:12. But Jesus changed all that.

"…And from the days of John the Baptist (Old Testament – Old Covenant under the Curse) **until now** (Jesus establishing taking back our authority under the Blessing) **the Kingdom of Heaven suffereth violence, and the violent take it** (back) **by force."**   **Matthew 11:12 (KJV)**

"And Jesus came and spake saying, 'All Power is given unto me in Heaven and Earth. Go Ye Therefore and Teach all Nations."   **Matthew 28:18 (KJV)**

"Then He called His twelve disciples together, and gave them power and authority over all devils and to cure diseases."   **Luke 9:1 (KJV)**

Granted, we find Scriptures in the New Testament that call us to pray and to petition God. But where are there any examples of this actually being done in regard to someone's healing or deliverance? Show me one miraculous healing or deliverance of any kind which resulted from the petitionary prayers of any other person. And even if one could say that it's implied they prayed, despite the fact that it does not say so, what does that prove but that I am still right? Let's say, in some of these instances that they did pray beforehand and we simply are not privy to it. Nevertheless, they were not healed until they were touched or commanded to be healed.

Here is one such 'almost exception': The raising of Lazarus from the dead. Jesus prays to the Father about what He is about to do. Note the prayer:

"Then they took away the stone from the place where the dead was laid. And Jesus lifted up His eyes, and said (prayed)**, 'Father, I thank Thee that Thou hast heard Me. And I knew that Thou hearest Me always: but because of the people which stand by I said it, that they may believe that Thou hast sent Me.' And when He thus had spoken, He cried with a loud voice, 'Lazarus, come forth.' And he that was dead came forth, bound hand and foot with grave clothes: and his face was bound about with a napkin. Jesus saith unto them, 'Loose him, and let him go."** John 11:41-44 (KJV)

Do you see how Jesus qualifies His prayer to the Father? "Father, I thank Thee that Thou HAST heard Me, and I KNEW that Thou hearest Me ALWAYS," He thanks God for hearing Him when? In the past tense, when Jesus said days before, "This sickness is not unto death," That's when!!! Jesus never prayed to the Father about raising Lazarus, He simply declared, "This sickness is not unto death!" And, the Father heard Him. So why is He praying now? Simple, read the next sentence, "But because of the people which stand by I said it, that they may believe that thou hast sent me." In effect, Jesus is saying, "OK, I am praying now Father, but not because I doubt My words or that You did not hear me the first time. Father, do not misconstrue this prayer as doubt, but understand I am only doing it for the benefit of those who are listening."

Ok, so I am going to make this real easy. I've done the homework for you. But, you are still obligated to draw your own conclusions based upon these scriptures. Following are all the recorded miracles found in the New Testament. You will see declarations, instructions, and laying on of hands. It's up to you to show me the petitionary prayers.

Included in each example is everywhere that particular miracle is recorded in the gospels. For context, the reader is encouraged to look up each reference. All that is given here is the healer's interaction with the subject of the miracle.

1. **Changing water to wine**   **Jn 2:7-8**

a. *Jesus said unto them, "Fill the water pots with water."*

b. *And He said unto them, "Draw out now, and bear unto the governor of the feast."*

2. **The Nobleman's son**   **Jn 4:50**

Jesus said, unto him, "Go your way; your son lives."

3. **The enormous catch of fish**   **Lk 5:4**

He said unto Simon, "Launch out into the deep, and let down your nets for a draught."

4. **Demoniac in the synagogue**   **Mk 1:25**   **Lk 4:35**

And Jesus rebuked him, saying, "Hold your peace, and come out of him."

5. **Peter's Mother-in law**   **Mt 8:15**   **Mk 1:31   Lk 4:39**

And He touched her hand, and the fever left her.

And He came and took her by the hand, and lifted her up; and immediately the fever left her.

And He stood over her, and rebuked the fever; and it left her.

6. **Healing of a leper**   **Mt 8:3**   **Mk 1:41   Lk 5:13**

And Jesus put forth His hand, and touched him, saying, "I will; be thou clean."

7. **Healing one paralyzed**   **Mt 9:2,6**   **Mk 2:3   Lk 5:18**

a. *"Son, be of good cheer; your sins be forgiven you"*

b. *"Arise, take up your bed, and go unto your house."*

8. **The sick man by the pool**   Jn 5:6,8

    a. He said unto him, "Will you be made whole?"

    b. Jesus said unto him, "Rise, take up your bed, and walk."

9. **The withered hand**   Mt 12:13   Mk 3:5   Lk 6:10

    Then said He to the man, "Stretch forth your hand." And he stretched it forth, and it was restored whole.

10. **Centurion's servant**   Mt 8:13   Lk 7:9

    And Jesus said unto the Centurion, "Go your way; and as you have believed, so be it done unto you."

11. **The widow's son**   Lk 7:13-14

    He said unto her "weep not," and He came and touched the bier and they who bear him stood still. And He said, "Young man, I say unto you, Arise."

12. **Demoniac**   Mt 12:22   Lk 11:14

    Then was brought unto Him one possessed with a devil, blind, and dumb: and He healed him.

13. **The storm**   Mt 8:26   Mk 4:39   Lk 8:24

    Then He arose, and rebuked the winds and the sea; and there was a great calm.

    And He arose, and rebuked the wind, and said unto the sea, "Peace, be still."

14. **Casting out Legion**   Mt 8:32   Mk 5:8,9,13   Lk 8:26

    And He said unto them, "Go."

    For He said unto him, "Come out of the man, you unclean spirit." and He asked him, "What is your name?" And forthwith He gave them leave.

15. **Jairus' daughter** Mt 9:24-25 Mk 5:41 Luke 8:41

a. He said unto them, "Give place: for the maid is not dead, but asleep."

b. He took her by the hand, and the maid arose.

c. And He took the damsel by the hand and said unto her, "Talitha cumi;" which is being interpreted, "Damsel, I say unto you, arise."

16. **Healing of Hemorrhage** Mt 9:22 Mk 5:34 Lk 8:48

But Jesus turned Him about, and when He saw her, He said, "Daughter, be of good comfort;thy faith hath made thee whole."

17. **Blind Men** Mt 9:28

And Jesus saith unto them, "Believe ye that I am able to do this?" They said unto Him, "Yea Lord." Then touched He their eyes, saying, "According to your faith be it unto you."

18. **Feeding Five Thousand** Mt 14:19 Mk 6:41 Lk 9:12 Jn 6:5

He commanded the multitude to sit down on the grass, and took the five loaves, and the two fishes, and looking up to Heaven, He blessed, and brake, and gave the loaves to His disciples, and the disciples to the multitude.

19. **Walking on the Water** Mt 14:25 Mk 6:49 Jn 6:19

And in the fourth watch of the night Jesus went unto them, walking on the sea

20. **Daughter of Syrophenician** Mt 15:28 Mk 7:25

Then Jesus answered and said unto her, "O woman, great is thy faith: be it unto thee even as thou wilt."

21. **Feeding 4,000** Mt 15:36 Mk 8:8

And He took the seven loaves and fishes, and gave thanks, and brake them, and gave to his disciples, and the disciples to the multitude.

22. **Deaf and Dumb**   **Mk 7:33-34**

And He took him aside from the multitude, and put His fingers into his ears, and He spit, and touched his tongue; and looking up to

Heaven, He sighed, and saith unto him, "Ephphatha," that is , Be Opened.

23. **Blind man**   **Mk 8:23-25**

And He took the blind man by the hand, and led him out of the town; and when He had spit on his eyes, and put His hands upon him, He asked him if he saw ought. And he looked up, and said, "I see men as trees, walking." After that He put His hands again upon his eyes, and made him look up: and he was restored, and saw every man clearly.

24. **Demon possessed boy**   **Mt 17:14**   **Mk 9:23-25**   **Lk 9:38-43**

a.   *And Jesus rebuked the devil; and he departed out of him:*

b.   *Jesus said unto him, "If thou canst believe, all things are possible to him that believeth." And straightway the father of the child cried out, and said with tears, "Lord I believe; help thou mine unbelief." When Jesus saw that the people came running together, He rebuked the foul spirit, saying unto him, "Thou dumb and deaf spirit, I charge thee, come out of him, and enter no more into him."*

25. **Tribute Money**   **Mt 17:24**

"Go thou to the sea, and cast an hook, and take up the fish that first cometh up; and when thou hast opened his mouth, thou shalt find a piece of money: that take, and give unto them for me and thee."

26. **Healing woman w/spirit of infirmity**   **Lk 13:12-13**

"Woman, thou art loosed from thine infirmity." And He laid His hands on her, and immediately she was made straight.

27. **Healing a man with dropsy**   **Lk 14:1-4**

And He took him, and healed him, and let him go;

28. **Healing ten lepers**   **Lk 17:14**

And when He saw them, He said unto them, "Go shew yourselves unto the priests." And it came to pass, that, as they went they were cleansed.

29. **Raising Lazarus**   **John 11:4,11,15,23,25,41-43**

"This sickness is not unto death, but for the glory of God, that the Son of God might be glorified thereby."

"Our friend Lazarus sleepeth: but I go, that I may awake him out of sleep"

"Lazarus is dead, and I am glad for your sakes that I was not there, to the intent ye may believe; nevertheless let us go unto him."

"Thy brother shall rise again."

"I am the resurrection, and the life: he that believeth in Me, though he were dead, yet shall he live: And whosoever liveth and believeth in Me shall never die. Believest thou this?"

"Father, I thank Thee that thou hast heard me. And I knew that Thou hearest me always: but because of the people which stand by I said it. That they may believe that Thou hast sent Me."

"Lazarus, Come Forth."

30. **Blind Men**   **Mt 20:32-34**

And Jesus stood still, and called them, and said, "What will ye that I do unto you?" They say unto Him, "Lord that our eyes may be opened." So Jesus had compassion on them, and touched their eyes: and immediately their eyes received sight, and they followed Him.

31. **Healing of a blind man   Mk 10:51-52   Lk 18:41-42**

"What wilt thou that I shall do unto thee?"

"Receive thy sight: thy faith hath saved thee (made the whole)"

32. **Healing of a slave's ear   Lk 22:51**

And He touched His ear and healed Him.

33. **The fig tree   Mt 21:19**

"Let no fruit grow on thee henceforthward forever."

34. **Second catch of fishes   Jn 21:6**

"Cast the net on the right side of the ship, and ye shall find (fish)."

Miracles Performed by Disciples:

35. **By the Seventy   Luke 10:17**

And the seventy (disciples) returned again with joy, saying, "Lord, even the devils are subject unto us through they name."

36. **By Stephen   Acts 6:8**

And Stephen, full of faith and power, did great wonders and miracles among the people.

37. **By Philip   Acts 8:6-7**

And the people with one accord gave heed unto those things which Phillip spake, hearing and seeing the miracles which he did. For unclean spirits, crying with loud voice, came out of many that were possessed with them: and many taken with palsies, and that were lame, were healed.

38. **Lame Man**   **Acts 3:6**

"Silver and gold have I none; but such as I have give I thee: in the name of Jesus Christ of Nazareth rise up and walk." And he took him by the right hand, and lifted him up: and immediately his feet and ankle bones received strength.

39. **Death of Ananias and Sapphira**   **Acts 5:4-5, 9-10**

"Whiles it remained, was it not thine own? And after it was sold, was it not in thine own power? Why hast thou conceived this thing in

thine heart? Thou hast not lied unto men, but unto God." And Ananias hearing these words fell down, and gave up the ghost.

Then Peter answered unto her, "How is it that ye have agreed together to tempt the Spirit of the Lord? Behold, the feet of them which have buried thy husband are at the door, and shall carry thee out." Then fell she down straightway at his feet, and yielded up the ghost.

40. **Sick Healed**   **Acts 5:15**

They brought forth the sick into the streets, and laid them on beds and couches, that at the least the shadow of Peter passing by might overshadow some of them.

41. **Aeneas healed of Palsy**   **Acts 9:34**

And Peter said unto him, "Aeneas, Jesus Christ maketh thee whole: arise, and make thy bed."

42. **Dorcas**   **Acts 9:40**

But Peter put them all forth, and kneeled down, and prayed; and turning him to the body said, "Tabitha, arise."

43. **Elymas, the sorcerer, Blinded**   **Acts 13:11**

"And now, behold, the hand of the Lord is upon thee, and thou shalt be blind, not seeing the sun for a season."

44. **Lame Man Healed**   **Acts 14:10**

(Paul) steadfastly beheld him and perceived that he had faith to be healed. (He) said with a loud voice, "Stand upright on thy feet."

45. **Girl with Spirit of Divination**   **Acts 16:18, 19:11**

Paul, being grieved turned and said to the spirit, "I command thee in the name of Jesus Christ to come out of her."

46. **Eutychus Raised from Dead**   **Acts 20:10**

And Paul went down, and fell on him, and embracing him said, "Trouble not yourselves; for his life is in him."

47. **Bitten by a Viper**   **Acts 28:5**

And he (Paul) shook off the beast (viper) into the fire, and felt no harm.

48. **Father of Publius healed**   **Acts 28:8-9**

Paul entered in, and prayed, and laid his hands on him, and healed him. So when this was done, others also, which had diseases in the island, came, and were healed.

I hear the voices claiming the age old excuse that it was different for Jesus and His disciples. The opinion is, that they had some special dispensation which we do not possess. But, that is just another fine example of "buffet' line Christianity." In other words, going through the Word of God and picking from it only what you want, what is easy, and leaving the rest. We all (in the Christian church) agree to the importance of our own personal discipleship, and certainly our responsibility to the "Great Commission." We just don't necessarily accept the High Calling. Like most high callings, it's too difficult, particularly the parts that require such great faith of us.

Mark 16: 15-18

And He (Jesus) **said unto them** (His Disciples)**, "Go ye into all the world, and preach the gospel to every creature. He that believeth and is baptized shall be saved; but he that believeth not shall be damned.** (and this is how you will be able to tell if they really believe or not) **And these signs shall follow them that believe;**

1. **In my Name shall they cast out devils;**
2. **they shall speak with new tongues;**
3. **They shall take up serpents;**
4. **and if they drink any deadly thing, it shall not hurt them;**
5. **they shall lay hands on the sick, and they shall recover." (KJV)**

It's important to get this. Jesus is talking to His disciples as He is preparing to commission them. He is telling them that in the future, people will be saved because they will believe on Him through them. Furthermore, He instructs them on how to know if those people (in the future) genuinely believe or not. He says it will be clearly evident: **"(these signs shall follow them that believe; In my Name shall they cast out devils; they shall speak with new tongues; They shall take up serpents; and if they drink any deadly thing, it shall not hurt them; they shall lay hands on the sick, and they shall recover)."**

How do we know someone is from God and that they believe? How do we know that we are from God in order to believe ourselves? Believers are known by their fruit. They are known by what their belief produces. Our faith is known by its works. Who are these people that will believe, through the disciples, in the future? You and me, that's who!! If we believe, that is! It might be quite natural then to ask oneself the question, "do I really believe?" Well if these miraculous signs are not evident in my life, then the answer seems fairly obvious. This was the question I had to examine my own heart and life with. In being honest with myself, it was clear that none of these things were evident in my life. Therefore, only one conclusion could be drawn: "I did not believe."

"Verily, verily, I say unto you, 'He that believeth on me, the works that I do shall he do also; and greater works than these shall he do; because I go unto my Father. And whatsoever ye shall ask in my name, that will I do, that the Father may be glorified in the Son. If ye shall ask any thing in My name, I will do it." **John 14:12-14 (KJV)**

Once again, a person has to be honest with themselves, "Do I really believe?" Here Jesus says people who believe are evidenced by this fact: They will do the works He did. Furthermore, they will do even greater works than Him. To date, I have yet to raise someone from the dead, walk on water, or give sight to a blind man. On the basis of Jesus' words here, I must conclude that I have a ways to go. That being said though, the fact remains that despite my lack of faith, I am pressing forward in faith, and nurturing it daily. As long as I continue to press in, these goals of faith will inevitability manifest themselves. I know one day these signs and greater will be as normal a part of my day as the rising of the sun.

"And the Lord said, 'If ye had faith as a grain of mustard seed, YE MIGHT SAY unto this sycamine tree, Be thou plucked up by the root, and be thou planted in the sea; AND IT SHOULD OBEY YOU." Luke 17:6 (KJV)

Note here, Jesus says if we had faith no bigger than a mustard seed, we could tell a sycamine tree what to do and **it would obey us**. First note He said it would obey <u>US</u>. If we command it (in faith) it would obey us. Then note, if trees or mountains are not obeying us, our faith must be *smaller* than a mustard seed. Not sure how big a mustard seed is? Let me show you. It is about the size of this period. (.) So, let's not kid ourselves about our faith. On the other hand, lets embrace the challenge and choose to grow in belief.

"For verily I say unto you, 'That whosoever shall say unto this mountain, Be thou removed, and be thou cast into the sea; and shall not doubt in his heart, but shall believe that those things which he saith shall come to pass; he shall have whatsoever he saith. Therefore I say unto you, what things soever ye desire, when ye pray, believe that ye receive them, and ye shall have them." Mark 11:23-24 (KJV)

Look to Luke 17:6, and you will see Jesus saying it again. Note: "Whosoever, shall SAY unto this mountain." Who is 'whosoever'? Simply whoever believes, that's who. If you believe, then whosoever is you. And if you had faith at least the size of a mustard seed, the mountain would obey you. Note, that it must be said, "with no doubt." If you believe that what you say will happen, then it will. It's as simple as that! Also note once again, He never says anything about praying for the mountain to move, anymore than He said to pray for the sycamine tree to move.

"Verily I say unto you, 'Whatsoever ye shall bind on earth shall be bound in Heaven: and whatsoever ye shall loose on earth shall be loosed in Heaven."

Matthew 18:18 (KJV)

Here are the facts. No one can heal someone simply by saying, "Be healed." If that were possible, we would not need doctors anymore. One cannot wish away sickness or injury, one cannot think themselves positively out of legs that don't work and into legs that do work. Only God can cause such things to be so, and those whom He empowers through the Holy Spirit to do the same. Here in Matthew 18:1, He declares that we are in charge on the earth. If we say something is acceptable, then He will back us up. If we say something is unacceptable, He will back us up. We have the authority purchased by Christ, and He has the power.

Therefore, when speaking healing or deliverance into someone, we have the authority to say what will happen. If God is not with us, then nothing will happen. If something does happen, then we can only conclude that God is with us. Remember Jesus words, "If you won't believe what I say, believe what I do." In other words, anyone can say they are from God, but you might say, "The proof is in the pudding," so to speak. Saying you are sent from God is one thing, doing what God does is another thing entirely.

So, then what is the place of petitionary prayer? I am going to have to assume the reader paid attention in Sunday school so we don't have to recite all the scriptures about prayer. Knowing the need for prayer is no big news flash. But what is the proper place of petitionary prayer? It is important to say something about it here so that no one misunderstands the preceding comments. Petitionary prayer has its place. The time that the Lord and I have together often involves requests on my part, directed toward Him. During those times, God has requests of me as well. That's right, God petitions me for things just as much as I do Him. This sounds odd, but it's true.

Every Christian has to come to terms with the fact that there are things God asks of us. In this way, prayer time is our opportunity to share our concerns together. From these conversations He acts upon my requests that are His to handle. In like manner, I act upon things that are mine to handle. It's not so different than sitting down with my wife and going over the business of life. By doing so, we get on the same sheet of music and are able to act intelligently upon the desires of our mate (and vice versa).

Having done this, when the time comes to address the need, we don't have to have a long conversation about it. The fact is, we already know what to do. I know where she stands, she knows where I stand. With Jesus raising Lazarus, there a clear implication that Jesus and the Father were completely in sync as to what was going to happen. Simply declaring the obvious was all that was left to do.

My bride does not call me every time a little decision needs to be made, nor do I call her about simple matters that we are already in agreement over. In the business of life, we already know what needs to be done and that our mate is in agreement with us concerning it. Imagine how annoying it would be to have your wife call you at work to ask if she should buy bread at the store; then run through all the bread options she is looking at. If we have not got that detail worked out after 27 years of marriage, we certainly have bigger issues.

I'm not implying that God would be annoyed with me if I did the same thing to Him, because we know that there is no concern too small for God. What I am attempting to say is that if I don't already know what to do about the basic business of bringing life to others, as He would have it, then I really need to go back to Sunday school and pay attention this time. When someone is sick, maimed, hurt, or broken hearted, I don't really have to seek counsel with God to know if I should reach out and make things right. That is NOT to say, I don't confer with Him. Walking in the Spirit means I should already be able to know the mind of the Father on any given matter, and what is best for the situation at hand.

Here is something else. I only ask God ONCE for a prayer request. After that, I rightfully assume I have what I asked for, even if it has yet to manifest itself to my physical senses. God always keeps His promises, and it is impossible for Him to not give me what I have asked for according to His will and His Word, in faith. He has bound Himself to His own Word. And He does so to such extent that He *is* His Word. Therefore, rather than asking until I receive it, I thank Him until I receive it. In other words, I assume He has given it to me already, and so I thank Him for it. Remember what Jesus just said while praying for Lazarus, "I thank you for hearing me, as you always hear me." Recall also I John 5:14-15

"And this is the confidence <u>that we have IN Him</u>, that, if we ask anything according to His will, He heareth us: And if we KNOW that He hears us, whatsoever we ask, <u>we KNOW that we HAVE</u> (present tense) the petitions that we desired of Him." **1 John 5:14-15 (KJV)**

We KNOW He always hears us, so we also KNOW we HAVE whatever we have asked for. To continue to petition God for something already asked for implies a whole lot of things. It certainly implies that we have not gotten it yet, that He did not hear me the first time, that He does not care nor want to give it to me, or that for some reason He said no. It implies that God is not a good God... that He actually could want someone to stay sick or in bondage. It also implies we are convinced we have to persuade Him like a child does his parents at a candy store. It implies that for all our words, maybe we can get Him to give us what we want if we keep saying, "please, please, please, please," while stomping our feet. It implies many other things as well. Mostly though, it just says that we are only "hoping" to get what we asked for, we are full of doubt, and we don't expect to have what we asked for. Above all it says, "We have no faith."

It is a simple fact, we don't get what we want, we only get what we expect. If we want it bad enough then, we will have to KNOW God, understand Him, seek Him, and learn to expect, not hope.

"He that spared not His own Son, but delivered Him up for us all, how shall He not with Him also freely give us ALL things?" **Romans 8:32 (KJV)**

Don't misunderstand, it's not that we should stop knocking or seeking for the manifestation of our request, rather we must do as one does who knows they have already received it. Thanksgiving before receiving frustrates the devil and his ability to tempt us to doubt. Just stop asking Him to do something you know He has already done. Instead choose to believe. When you do, it will be very apparent because you are already grateful for something you have yet to see with your eyes.

"Blessed are those who have not seen, and yet believe." **John 20:29 (KJV)**

People rightfully think the trouble is us not knowing what God's will is on a given matter. We all understand if our request is outside of God's will, He is not going to produce it. It's as simple as that. This is not a bad thing, this is a good thing. That is trusting God to know what is best for us. Unfortunately, we are convinced that God's will is unknowable. Well, that is just ignorance gone to seed. His will is far from being a secret. He could not possibly be any more clear than He already has been. What is revealed when someone says they don't know God's Will on a matter, is that they do not read their Bible. Furthermore, it reveals they rely upon circumstances and what other people have attempted to teach them, to understand God. God always says what He means and means what He says. Therefore, find out what He says about you. Believe it and RECEIVE it as your own. What could anyone possibly have to lose by embracing faith?

"And the disciples came, and said unto Him, 'Why speakest Thou unto them in parables?' He answered and said unto them, 'BECAUSE IT IS GIVEN UNTO YOU TO KNOW THE MYSTERIES OF THE KINGDOM OF HEAVEN, BUT TO THEM IT IS NOT GIVEN. <u>For whosoever hath, to him shall be given, and he shall have more abundance: but whosoever hath not, from him shall be taken away even that he hath</u>.

Therefore speak I to them in parables: because they seeing see not; and hearing they hear not, neither do they understand. And in them is fulfilled the prophecy of Esaias, which saith, By hearing ye shall hear, and shall not understand; and seeing ye shall see, and shall not perceive: For this people's heart is waxed gross, and their ears are dull of hearing, and their eyes they have closed; lest at any time they should see with their eyes, and hear with their ears, and should understand with their heart, and should be converted, and I should heal them. But blessed are your eyes, for they see: and your ears, for they hear. For verily I say unto you, That many prophets and righteous men have desired to see those things which ye see, and have not seen them; and to hear those things which ye hear, and have not heard them."   **Matthew 13:10-17 (KJV)**

Here is one thing I know. God wants to bless us with the desires of our heart. He wants to bless us as any godly husband wants to bless his wife. Just this morning my wife and I were talking about this. I told her that for some time I have been practicing doing for her what God does for me. That is saying "Yes," to her as much as possible. A husband who says "Yes," to his wife's requests with eagerness, is a blessing to her soul.

God makes promises, so that He can keep them. That's why He makes them. I never made promises to my wife on our wedding day to break them, I made them to keep them. I did not do it to bind myself to her, I made them to prove how much I really did love her. They were not empty words, and I can prove it. It's been twenty five years, and I mean them more now than I did then. Nor did I say, "Hey, let's try this marriage thing and see how it works out." I told her exactly how it was going to work out ahead of time. "I am going to love, serve, protect, and provide for you for the rest of your life 'PERIOD!'"

If I being evil compared to God could do such a thing, imagine how "MUCH MORE" we should expect from God. How is it wrong for my bride to expect me to keep my promises to her? Not wrong at all. She should be able to safely and securely trust me and my love for her for the rest of her life. Shall we expect less of God's promises to us? I think not.

In my experience, there is no question that the most effective prayers of faith are the spontaneous ones. Usually, these "flair prayers" are from the heart, and pack a punch of force. I have many times rejected long-winded prayer, in favor of a quick statement. Then I would immediately redirect my attention elsewhere, to prevent doubt from creeping in. For example, there was a couple we know who were being attacked severely by demonic forces. It seemed everyday their physical and emotional condition progressively worsened. When it finally got to the point where their very lives were being threatened; we felt compelled to ask for permission to heal them. We were convinced that if we did not step in, all would be lost.

They come from a very conservative "old school" Christian background that discourages getting all worked up with the kind of faith that heals people. Every time we spoke to them about healing, they flatly rejected it. It was their opinion that all such suffering comes from God and should be received as such. The absurdity of this doctrine was clearly identified when we asked them this time, "Well, if it's God's will and purpose for you to suffer, why are you not praying for more suffering? I mean if you can learn so much from this, imagine what you could learn from more."

In many Christian's mind it's acceptable to pray to be healed in a hopeful manner, but not in a faith-filled manner. This too is absurd. If it's God's will for people to suffer, then we are contradicting and praying against God's will when we pray for healing or deliverance for anyone. The plain truth about this doctrine is that it's much easier to have faith that bad things will happen than good things. Again, it's much easier to have faith in the devil's power than in God's. And so the carnage continues... For many believe the simplest way to avoid disappointment, is to never expect anything good.

This particular couple had finally gotten sick and tired of being sick and tired, though. Healing was starting to sound much better than suffering. Their long held doctrine was not making as much sense to them as it had when they were not dying. Finally, they invited us to their home. We sat down with them, and spoke to them briefly about faith and healing. Then, I did exactly what God told me to do. I looked the husband in the eye and asked, "Do you want to be healed?" He said, "Yes, I do." I stood up, put my hand on his shoulder, and said, "Ok, you are healed." Then I turned to his wife and asked, "Do you want to be healed?" She said, "Yes, I do." I placed my hand on her shoulder and said "Ok, you are healed." Then I turned to Belle and said, "Ok, Sweetheart it's time to go." She got up, and out the door we went without another word. I imagine this was probably quite anti-climactic for a couple who was accustomed to long petitionary prayers.

When we got in the car, my wife asked why I had been so quick and left abruptly. I said, "To not leave a moment's opportunity to doubt." People get into long pleading prayers, and I have in the past as well. Pleading prayers are laden with loads of doubt. By implication, we are attempting to persuade God to do something; for all our words. Nowhere in all the healings in the Gospels and in Acts, do you see such prayers. Rather, you see simple ones like this, "Silver and gold, have I none, but such as I do have I give to you; rise up and walk." This same couple now is healthier than they have been in years. They are completely healed and delivered of the threats against their lives. The truth is known by what it produces.

On another occasion, there was this woman who confided that she was on her way to see the doctor. Apparently, she had been advised that she had a painful ectopic pregnancy, and the embryo would have to have a D&C surgery to remove it from the fallopian tube. In coming to us, she was clearly distraught by this evil report. Obviously, there was not enough time to teach her about faith. This baby's life was at stake. Taking her hand in mine, I looked earnestly into her eyes and said, "The baby is fine, and there will be no problem. Go see your doctor today, because he will have good news for you. Oh, and this baby…this baby will be great in the Kingdom of Heaven." The next day, she contacted me to say that the doctors were amazed. Apparently the baby had dislodged itself after all and was growing safely in the uterus, completely healthy.

The longer a person thinks about the object of their faith-filled prayer, the more "self" gets mixed into it. To heal or to fix any situation, simply state what must be. After which, it is essential to turn our mind to other things. This is not what I do in every situation. Nevertheless, considerable observation of past results indicates that these type of prayers have been (by far) the most effective.

I hear you asking the question, "So, why not do it that way every time?" Well, you are then speaking of formulas. That is, "ways of doing things that work." The trouble is, God consistently defies our formulas. Healing is not about methodologies, it's about doing as we are told. In other words, we do not heal people. We never have, and we never will. Only the Holy Spirit heals people. It's just that He flows through us to accomplish that end; in the same manner He flowed through Jesus. Therefore, healing can only flow through us if we do as He tells us to do. Formulas put us in charge of situations. It leaves us overestimating our part in things and underestimating His.

"Then laid they their hands on them, and they received the Holy Ghost. And when Simon saw that through the laying on of the apostles' hands the Holy Ghost was given, he offered them money, saying, 'give me also this power, that on whomsoever I lay hands, he may receive the Holy Ghost.' But Peter said unto him, 'Thy money perish with thee, because thou hast thought that the gift of God may be purchased with money. Thou hast neither part nor lot in this matter: for thy heart is not right in the sight of God."

Acts 8:17-21 (KJV)

Other things which have been overcome in our lives:

The Flu

The flu used to nail me several times a year. It was always horrible, and unavoidable. The kids would usually be the ones to bring it home. No more had they walked in the door with it, than it would hit me like a ton of bricks; and put me down for the better part of a week. All I could do was lay on the bathroom floor praying someone would just come and put me out of my misery. When praying for healing did not work, praying for death seemed the next best thing. In between puking up my guts, I begged and pleaded with God for either life or death, never getting either.

One day, after the clearing process represented in these first visions had begun, our pastor told the congregation how he had not been sick in over twenty years. Furthermore, he described the faith process he had gone through to obtain this victory. By the end of the church service, I also decided to never be sick again for the rest of my life. It wasn't long before this resolve was put to the test. One weekend, I was scheduled to drive a few hundred miles on business. Of all the times for it to happen, the flu had to pick that time to hit me like a high speed freight train.

This time was different though. For the first time in my life, I was armed with the Sword (the Word) to resist the attack. I stayed up all night before, pacing the house praying, reading and speaking God's word, resisting the sickness, the devil, and the temptation to doubt God's Word. My body was so weak it was nearly impossible to stand. Nevertheless, I refused to sit or lie down the whole night. My body screamed, "Please let me lie down and die in peace." I refused, rather making it stumble back and forth across the living room floor all night long. The next morning, the symptoms (temptations) still hung heavy over me. What to do about the trip now became the question. The healing had already happened (because I asked for it). I reasoned now that I was only dealing with the temptation to not believe it. Therefore if I truly believed, then it would be evident by works.

"And this is the confidence that we have in Him, that, if we ask anything according to His will, He heareth us: And if we know that He hear us, <u>whatsoever we ask</u>, we <u>KNOW</u> that we <u>HAVE</u> the petitions that we desired of Him." **1 John 5:14-15 (KJV)**

"<u>Even so faith, if it hath not works</u>, is dead, being alone. Yea a man may say, 'Thou hast faith, and I have works:' shew me thy faith without thy works, and <u>I will shew thee my faith by my works</u>. Thou believest that there is one God; thou doest well: the devils also believe and tremble. But wilt thou know, O vain man, that <u>faith without works is dead</u>." **James 2:17 (KJV)**

In other words, if I had just been healed, then my actions would show it! There would be works involved in my faith. It means, I would get up and do what I would do, as if I felt healed. I would believe God's Word *MORE* than the way I felt. With that in mind, by faith I took off on the trip. The whole way there, I felt horrible. Holding my stomach, I continued to resist and press on in faith. That evening, after arriving, I was miserable beyond belief. I shouted to the Lord, "God, I need a decisive blow against my adversary NOW!!!" God replied in an urgent tone. He said, "Think about your wife!!!" I obeyed and started to imagine her eyes, her hair, her smile...and other things. Not more than two minutes later, all symptoms (temptations) of the flu absolutely vanished. Suddenly, I felt normal and like I had never been sick in the first place. It was like it was all my imagination. I felt great. "Whoa!!!," I said in astonishment.

Here is what I learned. The symptoms (temptations) had consumed me, as a result of the fight over them. I was completely focused on the problem. My mind had entered into the battle to win. But, my strength was no match for the devil. We were both pushing and pushing with all our might in a heated deadlock. When I shouted out, God responded. He found the most effective distraction imaginable, that being my wife. Now her, I can focus on easily. The effect was one of me abruptly stepping aside. Have you ever had someone push against you with all their might? Equally matched means neither of you are able to move the other no matter what you do. But, if you suddenly step to the side, they fall flat on the floor. Well, the devil fell flat on his face that day.

The victory was won that day, but more attacks were soon to come. Fighting it out all night became quite common for a while. There was much to be encouraged about though. What had taken a week to overcome in the past, had been successfully reduced to about eight hours. There was not much sleep to be had on those nights. But, refreshment always came with the new day. The memory of my last battle with the flu is still vivid in my mind:

We were driving to a nearby town to do some shopping. It was normally a one hour drive. No more had we turned onto the highway though, than a nauseous feeling overtook me. There was no way I was going to let this attack stop us though. I was healed, and healed people go shopping. As we drove along though, it just kept getting worse. After driving about a half hour, I could not take it anymore. Pulling the car over, I asked Belle to drive while I walked down the shoulder of the highway; in front of the car. With the flashers going; she drove slowly behind me as I walked along slugging it out with the devil. After about a quarter of a mile, the symptoms (temptations) vanished. I got back in the passenger seat, and off we went rejoicing together over the victory.

After driving another five miles, however, the temptations returned in force. She stopped the car again, and I started walking once more. A few minutes later the temptations vanished, and I got back in the car again. A few miles later, they came back and she stopped the car again. This process went on for about five or six times. The last time was when I walked right up to the parking lot of the store, as she parked the car. Suddenly, the temptations (symptoms) vanished and never came back again. EVER. That was in 2004.

Death in an accident

The following event occurred quite some time ago. Even so, it remains as one of the most amazing and unexplainable miracles we ever witnessed. At that time in my life, I did not know anything about walking in the Spirit. Fortunately, my wife, Belle, did. Back then I relied entirely upon my sharp, analytical, and rational mind to get us through life. Had God's voice been available, there is no doubt the numerous cautions and warnings would have been evident to me. Had I even possessed enough respect for the Spirit, I may have at least listened to some of the cautions my wife as I prepared for the trip. Smart as I was though, I easily overcame all the warnings and cautions with my superior rational mind.

As the story goes, it was the summer of 1989 and we were in the process of moving from Nashville, Tennessee to Wasilla, Alaska. We were making the 5,000 mile trip in our 1986 Chevy half ton Silverado Truck. Behind us, we pulled a twenty foot enclosed trailer containing all our earthly possessions. With us, we also carried that which was most precious to us; our five month old daughter, Sierra.

Even before we left Nashville, Belle expressed growing concern that something was not right. She had this foreboding sense that something bad was going to happen, and had felt it for a couple of months. This spirit stuff made no sense to me, so I dismissed it with logic and reason. Being the good wife, she relented to follow her husband into peril.

Mistake one: Not listening to my wife.

Mistake two: The trailer's weight exceeded the safety limits of our truck.

Mistake Three: Rather than downsizing, I determined another way to mitigate the risk. At about 55 mph, the trailer would begin to sway badly. Being as smart as I was, this was easily overcome by keeping our speed under 55 mph.

Mistake four: Directly endangering the life of my daughter. Sierra was miserable in her car seat. She just could not get to sleep. She cried and cried, non-stop. When there seemed to be no other way, I overcame all my cautions and placed her on a mattress behind us. It seemed safe enough. It all seemed good and sensible. The moment we laid her down, she fell right to sleep.

Mistake Five: Deciding to drive at night. Traffic was heavy and had been backing up behind us. In order to avoid traffic, we decided to drive at night. It was a rational choice that made sense to me. About seventy-five miles out of Saint Louis, we were driving very early in the morning. I was getting sleepy and Belle was appealing to me to let her drive.

Mistake Six: Letting my wife, who hadn't often driven my truck nor towed a trailer, take over the driving. It was a rational conclusion that being drowsy was more dangerous than her inexperience.

Coaching her along, I showed her how to handle the truck. In particular, I showed her how to keep it slow and how to gear down when cresting a hill. Being fairly confident she was doing ok, I dozed off. As I slept, Belle says the cab of the truck filled with a very intense and destructive spiritual presence. She sensed very clearly that there was an eminent threat against us. It was so intense she spoke out against those spirits and the threat. She went on to bind them and declare that "they could not hurt her, her husband, or her baby, In Jesus Name!"

At that very moment, she just happened to be starting down a steep grade without having first slowed down. As the truck began picking up speed, the trailer began to sway back and forth. I awoke to Belle screaming that she could not stop it. I bolted upright and told her to pump the brakes. Unfortunately it was already too late. No more had I said that, than a big tractor trailer went past us doing about 70 or 80 mph. The air current from his trailer caught ours, and that was all it took. (On our right side was a 300 foot drop off into oblivion and on the left side was a rock wall). She lost control and the trailer whipped us completely around. Turning to look out my passenger side window, I saw this rock wall coming right at me. I flinched away from it in the last second. As we slammed up against the rock wall, my window exploded.

Instinctively we both whipped around to look in the back for our daughter. Belle screamed, "MY BABY!!!" This is what we saw in that millisecond of a flash. Everything in the back was gone, the mattress was gone, the bed of the truck was crushed, and all that was left of the trailer was the frame. Our precious daughter was gone amongst all that debris. In the next millisecond, we scrambled down out of the truck to search for her.

Mistake Seven: Relying on the laws of nature to determine the wellbeing of our daughter. Because I was the only one with any logical presence of mind, I had already concluded that our daughter was in pieces. Logic and reason dictated that there was no way she could have escaped being torn to bits. Not through all that tearing and exploding aluminum, glass, and other equally dangerous projectiles. Relying on my instinctive understanding of physics, I naturally headed around to the rear of the truck where the momentum and impact had carried everything. When I got to the rear of the truck, I saw debris scattered for hundreds of yards. It appeared as if a large plane had just crashed. Everything stretched from the point of impact, and off in a straight line for about three hundred yards.

At that instant I was stopped abruptly by something I did not expect; the sound of a baby crying. My wife in a panic and having asked the Lord where to go, had gone around to the front of the truck. Again, note: everything else we owned had followed the natural law of physics. Even amidst all this trauma, I knew exactly what to expect. So, how was it then that our baby was alive, and why was her cry coming from beyond the front of the truck?

I turned on my heels, and ran to the front. When I got there, I saw my wife standing about forty yards away and holding our daughter in her arms. Running up to her, I gathered up our baby in my arms. She was still so tiny, hardly bigger than a loaf of bread. The first thing I noticed was that she was in one piece and very much alive. The next thing I noticed was a small bit of blood on the corner of her lip.

Mistake Eight: Always expecting the worst. Since I did not know anything about my power, authority, or how to expect miracles, and as I still had no confidence in the goodness of God's Will, I concluded that our daughter had internal injuries. On closer examination however, it turned out that she had a small cut on the corner of her lip. She probably got it from the crab grass that she landed in. I wiped the blood from her lip and she was fine.

I had not even yet begun to ask myself how she got to where she was. But here it is: Somehow, she had got out from under the all the metal of the truck and topper when it all exploded. Rather than being carried away in pieces with everything else, she was thrown over the top of the truck and approximately 40 yards in front of us. Furthermore, she landed on the shoulder of the interstate on the only clump of crabgrass (only big enough to cradle a baby) in a long expanse of sharp gravel.

Realizing she was ok, I looked over my shoulder to see what was left of our truck. There was not much, that was certain. It was completely destroyed. Suddenly, smoke began billowing from under the hood. Clearly, the battery was shorting out. The topper had been wired for power, to run lights and a fan. When the topper had ripped from the bed of the truck, it had shorted out the wiring.

Quickly passing our baby to Belle, I ran back to the truck. Reaching behind the driver seat, I pulled out one of the fire extinguishers. Unfortunately, the hood of the truck was so crushed it would not open beyond the little catch inside. At that point, I attempted to spray through the bit of gap that there was. The fire did go out momentarily. After the extinguisher was expended though, the fire took off again. While attempting to reach under the seat for the other extinguisher, flames burst out from under the dash. The truck burning was inevitable now.

As this realization struck me, the age old question flashed across my mind. "If your house caught fire, what would you take with you on your way out the door?" My wallet, with absolutely all the money we had to our name, was sitting on the dash. Giving up on the extinguisher, I attempted to reach through the flames for my wallet. However at that instant, the flames erupted into a blaze. Then, the next thought to burst upon my mind was that all my firearms, along with ammunition, were right behind the seat. In addition, the truck had two full gas tanks, as well as propane bottles for camping, on board. Suddenly, I realized the truck was about to blow up.

Abandoning any hope of retrieving my wallet, I slammed the door, ran up the road, grabbed my new bride by the hand, told her the truck was going to blow up, and together we ran about four hundred yards up the interstate. The moment we turned around, the first explosion went off as the fuel tank was breached. It was just like in the movies. The whole truck came up off the ground, and then slammed back onto the pavement. Less than a minute later, the second tank blew. Once again, the entire vehicle was lifted off the ground. Then the ammunition started going off.

Imagine this scene. The truck has its driver side front tire on the white line, so it's obviously right on the road. It's early in the morning and pitch dark. The truck has just undergone two catastrophic explosions. Bullets are flying everywhere and shrapnel, from the explosions, is going in all directions. Nevertheless, there were idiots in cars zooming past on the freeway as if nothing was happening. I distinctly remember thinking how insensitive it was that people would not stop to see if they could render assistance. Seriously, back home we would stop if someone had a flat tire. I also remember thinking that they were going to get killed in the process of their depraved indifference and blame me for it. About ten minutes later, the first person finally stopped. He was a big burly truck driver. After calling in the emergency, he came to see if we were ok.

My wife had no shoes on, so he went back to his truck and got a pair of his. She does not normally wear size 13 men's shoes, but we were still very grateful. He continued to stand there with us, watching our lives burn away, until the emergency vehicles showed up.

As daybreak came, about forty-five minutes after the accident, the first emergency vehicle arrived. By then, there was not much to do other than clean up the mess. My back hurt a little, so they put me on a back board. As a precaution, they put our 5 month old on a back board for infants. It wrapped around her, making her look like she was in a cocoon. The ambulance took us to a small hospital in Fulton, Missouri (Misery). There, I lay on a sheet of plywood for a couple hours waiting for doctors to check us out. Lying there, during that time, all I could do was… breathe and move my eyes. Out of the corner of my eye, I could see my beautiful new bride holding our precious little sweetie in her plastic cocoon. Rather than talking to God, for some reason I began to talk to the devil. Tears flowed from my eyes. I said, "You want all our stuff so bad, you can have it. Between you and me, everything that is important to me is standing right over there."

Mistake Nine: Conceding to loss. Despite the fact that God had preserved our family, according to the words my wife spoke, we both made a similar mistake. We have since learned the importance of denying access to the devil of anything and everything that is ours. She had saved our lives, true enough, with her words and her faith (no thanks to me at all). Had she understood then what she understands now, she could have just as easily saved everything else as well. And I, though still possessing everything truly important to me; have since learned to not allow anything that is ours pass to our adversary. (PERIOD!!!) We both have come a long ways in this regard. It is a true fact if you give the devil an inch, he will try to take a mile.

While sorting the whole thing out in my mind, I watched my wife standing there about twenty feet away. She was so beautiful. "How could I let this happen to her?" Then, I just began praising the Lord. This experience was already teaching me that there is always a way that makes sense to a man, but the end thereof is his own destruction. All the sudden my best ideas, logic, and reason did not make all that much sense anymore. I began to see things the way God sees them. I began to see what was really valuable; I began to grow up real fast.

While it would still be many more years and much more adversity before I learned how to get control of my life, this moment was nevertheless the beginning of the end of "me." (From this point on, the adversity would just get worse and worse until we turned forty years old.)

Eventually, we were released with clean bills of health. We had no injuries whatsoever. As we walked down this long corridor, to leave the hospital, I held my wife's hand. She carried our little girl in her other arm. Here I was, as a husband and a father, with no idea what we were going to do the moment we walked out those doors. We had no money, no clothes, no place to go, and no way to get there if we did.

As we drew near the doors, a woman came walking in. Stopping in front of us, she introduced herself. "I heard you guys are not having such a great day," she said. "Yeah, you could say that," I responded in a monotone voice. "I represent a local ministry called 'Serve Ministries,' and we would like to know if we can get you a room at the motel? We would also like to get you guys some dinner, and new clothes," she stated warmly. Being still in a state of shock, all I could do was mutter "Yes, that would be nice. Thank you." They did all that, and ended up putting us up in a motel for nearly a week. They also took care of our meals, and new clothes.

So often people hear me challenging them to be the miracle everyone else is praying for. Had that woman and those people not been the miracle that day, it evades my imagination to wonder what would have become of us. This was step one in our process of learning hospitality from other people's examples, and the importance of being a servant. The first night after the accident, I sat on the left corner of the bed with my head in my hands. My wife sat on the other corner with her head in her hands. That is the first time I have ever experienced the numb sensation of shock and despair.

Without going through the rest of the story, by the end of the week we were on our way again. Less than two weeks later, we arrived in Alaska. It would be wonderful to be able to say everything worked out. However, the job that waited for me was not there. We arrived in July of 1989. We got our first paycheck in March of the next year. Our first winter in Alaska, we were homeless and penniless...

In retrospect, when looking at this particular event several things are clearly apparent. I had no idea what I was doing. My wife saved our lives with her words, and somehow our five month old daughter was able to suspend the laws of physics. What happened that day is absolutely impossible in every universe except the spiritual one. The only rational explanation is that she was snatched away in the embrace of an Angel and laid gingerly into that clump of grass. When she rolled over, she cut her lip on the grass.

Possibly there is someone out there far smarter than me. If so, any other rational explanations are warmly welcomed. Failing that, one can only conclude that there is a God and that He is a rewarder of those who diligently seek Him. This conclusion then demands we answer this question, "How then should we live?" My daughter's life dictates this, there is no debate. While a person is free to make their own choices, we have no excuse. My daughter is alive because there is a God, and our god is God.

Mechanical problems fixed miraculously:

Here is another cool story. We used to have an old Ford truck. It was a one ton crew cab we had been driving for about thirteen years. By the time of this story, it had about 360,000 miles on it. To say it had been a very faithful truck for our family was a tremendous understatement. One day, we decided to go see the Harlem Globe trotters. They were performing in a town about two hours away. Belle had to work that day, so it was just me and the two older kids together on a beautiful Saturday.

We climbed into the truck, and took off in high spirits. About forty five minutes later, we had just passed through another nearby town and were heading down the interstate. Suddenly, the engine started making a huge thumping racket. It sounded like the rods were going to shoot through the heads at any moment! After pulling over, I tried to assess if there was something external that was causing the booming noise. Clearly it was not though. The engine was about to blow and that was all there was to it. It was not surprising in the least. I was not even upset about it. This truck had a good life, and it was time to put her down. However, it was very disappointing that we would not get to see the Harlem Globe Trotters.

Turning to the Austin and Sierra, I apologized and told them we needed to turn around and head back home. The tow bill was going to be very expensive. It seemed like a good thing to do to see how close we could get to home before it blew. Once it did, that would be the end of this old truck. We pulled up onto the next overpass to get turned around. While driving over the overpass though, I said out loud, "Wait a minute, I am going about this all wrong."

Sierra was sitting next to me and asked what I meant. Pulling over, I shut the engine off. Turning to the kids again I said, "Kids, I am sorry, I am doing this all wrong. I really want you to go see the Harlem Globe Trotters, and I know God does too. So, here is what we are going to do. We are going to pray over this truck and God is going to rebuild this engine for me, so we can go. After we are done praying for it, we are going to drive down the shoulder of this highway until we get to the turn off toward home (about two miles). If God rebuilds our engine by the time we get to that exit, we will turn back around and go see the Harlem Globe Trotters. They agreed, and so we prayed.

Then, we started down the road as I said we would. The engine was banging like crazy the whole way. As we bumped our way down the shoulder I prayed, "Lord, Belle and I have witnessed many miracles in our life. Our children believe you because of our stories. They are old enough now though, to see these miracles for themselves. God I am okay with this truck dying on us today. But, I am not okay with my kids missing out on the fun we had planned for them. God, please show them what you have showed us so many times." At that moment the turn off, the exit which headed us toward home, was right in front of us, so I engaged the turn signal. I kid you not... the instant I turned the steering wheel to the right to take the off ramp, the pounding, booming, thumping sound vanished completely!! The engine sounded like it was brand new.

My jaw dropped. Turning to my children, I saw that they were staring at me in astonishment. We all said a collective "Whoa!!!" At the end of the off-ramp, there was a gas station. I pulled in, and parked. As I shut the engine off, I was laughing. Our oldest daughter, Sierra, asked "Why are you laughing, Daddy?" I said, "Because sweetheart, I just love it when He does stuff like that." I started the engine again, shut it off again, and started it again several times. The engine sounded perfect every time.

Sierra had a friend back then that did not believe in God. She commented, "Daddy, why doesn't my best friend believe in God like we do?" I said, "Well my dear, most people require God to prove Himself before they will believe. But God has nothing to prove. We believe God before we see, and so He always gives us what we ask for." As true as God was to His word, I was true to mine. We headed off toward the Harlem Globe Trotters.

I loved that experience so much, it blessed me in ways that I continue to measure in the lives of our children to this day. We have had so many similar mechanical miracles over the years that I have kidded around about opening my own automotive repair shop and making a living from healing people's cars.

As we passed the place where the engine started making all the noise, Austin asked, "Daddy, is that the spot where the engine broke?" I replied, "Yes, it is, why do you ask?" He said, "Because one day I am going to be driving by this place with my children, and I am going to tell them about the time God rebuilt our engine. All the fireworks, on all the 4th of Julys that I have ever been to combined, could not begin to match the rejoicing in my spirit over what God had just done for my children.

We drove that truck for another six years. During that time, it also moved our entire household five more times. Finally, we sold it to a guy who lived in a nearby town. Every once in a while we would see it driving down the road. Whenever we did, we praised the Lord for His miracles and goodness to our family.

Amazing Grace

I used to have an old car that was always breaking down. It had been given the name, "Amazing Grace," as it was only amazing grace that kept it going. On a road trip during the winter, I got caught in an intense blizzard hundreds of miles from home. Visibility was down to about twenty five feet, at best. Consequently, 8-10 miles per hour was about as fast as the car could be driven. The truckers, on the other hand, whizzed by, insanely doing 45-50 miles an hour. This only decreased my visibility further, by the fury of snow that their trucks created in front of me. Nervously, I considered the possibility of one of them coming up behind me, and slamming into the back of my car. "Do they have radar or something?" I wondered, as I considered what it was that allowed them to travel so much faster than myself.

Suddenly, the engine on my car just died. No sputtering, no warning; it just died. Instantly, panic set in (I was younger then, and did not understand the things I understand now). Try as I might, the car would not restart. Was it out of gas? No, I had just filled the tank. I was freaking out! Any second now, a massive tractor trailer was going to slam into the back of my stalled car. What should I do? Abandon the car in the middle of the interstate? In the middle of a blizzard? Hmm, which would be better - dying of hypothermia (assuming a truck did not hit me when I stepped out of the car), or staying in the car to die from the impact of a truck colliding with my car? I shouted out, "God!!! You have to help me! If this car needs gas, give it some gas. Do whatever you have to do, but start this car!!!! Or, I will be dead in the next few moments," I took a deep breath, and turned the key one more time. It started!!! There was not even time for my customary "Whoa!!!" I just put the car in gear, and took off as fast as I could. Only when I was back up to speed did I rejoice and thank God for saving my life.

When the next exit came, I turned off the highway and pulled into a service station. Pulling up to the pump, I shut off the engine and attempted to top off the gas tank. It only took several gallons, and that was it. So, I popped the hood and looked at the engine. There staring me in the face, was a distributer wire unplugged and hanging off the side of the distributer. I plugged it back in, and started the engine. It ran perfectly. I thought to myself, how in the world did this engine start in this blizzard without electricity to the distributer? Whoa!!!" I could explain why the car died, but I could not explain how it had started. Oh, yes I could !!!

Bug Bites:

Some years ago we got called upon to deliver a woman who was suffering from severe demonic oppression. A friend of Belle's came to her and told her about a friend who was about to lose her children, and be put in a mental hospital. Apparently, she had a strange condition. She felt like she was being constantly bitten by thousands of little bugs… that did not exist. But these bugs, that did not exist, left visible marks all over her. She had been too many doctors, yet no one could help. They all said it was in her mind. We were her last resort. It only took a moment to assess the situation for what it really was, and we agreed to help. That evening I spent about an hour with the Lord, talking about her and getting instructions from Him on how to deal with it.

The next day Belle and I prayed over her, and ourselves. On our way, we stopped at our pastor's house. He and his wife covered us in prayer. When we arrived in her town, we pulled over and prayed some more. Then, we proceeded to her house. Upon arriving, we pulled in the driveway and got out. Starting at the driveway, we announced to the demonic residents who we were, why we were there, and what was going to happen today. Essentially, we gave them notice to pack their belongings, they were getting evicted. We started by walking the perimeter of the property, praying, and anointing each corner, (marking our territory with oil). Lastly, we anointed the door as we walked in.

The woman sat quietly at her kitchen table, as we seated ourselves beside her. We talked for a few moments and assessed that she did not understand what it meant to be God's child, and possibly wasn't saved. Furthermore, we were able to discover the process through which the evil spirits had come to torment her; mainly through a sinful relationship. We shared the whole gospel with her, and she invited Jesus into her life. Now having gained spiritual ownership for the Kingdom of Heaven, we were able to raise God's banner over her and her children. Laying hands on her, we began to rebuke the evil spirits. As we did so, her youngest son (about four years old) was standing about three inches from my right ear screaming at me to stop. He kept shouting that the Bible I had on the table "was not true". However, I refused to acknowledge his presence. The woman's responses continued to be soft and accepting. We were expecting a great deal more stress out of her, but it was not to be found. When we finished, we gave her instructions and then dismissed ourselves.

Everything was very calm, and we were pleased that it had gone so well. We got in the car, started the engine, and drove out of the driveway. The instant we hit the street, I started feeling this intense pricking all over my body that felt exactly like thousands of little bugs biting me! I told Belle, and we began to pray against it. Nevertheless, it continued all the way home. I called our pastor, and told him what happened. The moment he heard about them attacking me, they started also attacking him. "Whoa!!!" Now, He was feeling it as well. He said, "Hold on, let's join together and put an end to this." I agreed, and so he began to resist the enemy with me in prayer over the phone. We bound their power to touch us, in Jesus name, and rebuked them. After a couple minutes, the biting ceased abruptly. "Whoa !!!

Spider Bites

This talk of bug bites reminds me of another story. One day, I came across this lady I knew from the past. I was dismayed to see that she had one of her feet amputated. Wow, bad deal. She explained to me that she had been bitten by a brown recluse spider and it had gotten so bad the doctors had to take her foot. This event stunned me and I could not get it out of my mind for some time.

One day at work, I found myself in this situation where there were thousands of "daddy long-leg spiders" on this building. Apparently, they were having a "reproductive party." Some of us guys got to talking about how they are apparently one of the more poisonous spiders out there, but their mouth parts are so small and their legs so long that biting people is pretty difficult, if not impossible. We were goofing around and googling this rumor on the internet to see if there was any truth to it. The short of it was that I actually began to obsess about it, because there were so many of these spiders around.

A couple days later, while at work, I inadvertently smashed one with my arm. In doing so, it bit me! So much for the idea that they can't bite you. Immediately, the spot began to swell and discolor. I started to freak out. At that moment, God spoke up. "Ryker, what are you doing?", He asked. "What do you mean, Lord?" I replied. "Quit being so foolish, you know that spider can't hurt you. Nothing can hurt you." I knew He was attempting to remind me of Luke 10:19

"Behold, I give unto you power to tread on serpents and scorpions, and over all the power of the enemy: and nothing shall by any means hurt you."

Luke 10:19 (KJV)

I said, "You're right, Lord, I do know better than this. I am sorry. I admit to asking for this, by obsessing about fear rather than faith. I repent of this wicked sin of unbelief. I am so sorry, please forgive me." He agreed, and that was that. In less than one minute, the swelling and discoloration completely vanished.

Deliverance from "The Spirit of Rage"

There was this guy who came to me for counseling and mentorship, in regard to his failing marriage. Without telling the whole story, it quickly became very apparent there were some evil spirits who had taken up residence in him. Their presence and influence were causing all kinds of problems in his life. The main one manifested itself as the spirit of rage. It was this spirit, more than any other, which was primarily responsible for the marriage troubles. He dearly loved his wife, but he simply had no control over the rage.

We gained his consent to deliver him of these spirits and invited him over to our place. Following the direction of the Holy Spirit, we took him out to where I meet the Lord at night. There we seated him in a chair. My wife seated herself in a chair facing him. I stood behind him with my hands on his shoulders. Belle took his hands, and I started to pray over him. It was a rather calm and peaceful process, considering what we were engaged in doing. One by one I began naming the individual spirits, binding them up, and booting them out. Every time one left, our friend would shudder. His shoulders would heave, and then he would relax. I was saving the biggest spirit for last.

All during the process, he never said a single word. He seemed to not even be there, almost unconscious. Then the time came for the finale. Leaning over his shoulder, I whispered in his right ear. "Now for you, the biggest spirit of all. You know who you are, even without me saying your name. You think you are fearsome and powerful. I am going to show you though, you are nothing. I am not going to even speak your name. Nor will I even speak to you above a whisper and you will still do exactly as I say."

Suddenly the man started flailing around wildly and growling fiercely at me. He never used a single word, just growled and roared. For all his flailing around though, he did not even have the power to move his arms, nor remove himself from his seat. It was as if he were strapped down to the chair and was vainly trying to escape.

For a moment I was concerned about Belle. She was holding his hands and was only inches from his face. However, the Spirit told me to not be concerned. So I continued. Whispering in his ear again I said, "I am going to give you one chance to leave of your own free will. You may go right now and no harm will come to you. If you do not come out of him however, I will make you leave. Your hands and feet will be bound, you be gagged, and you be confined in darkness until the day of your judgment. If you do not come out of him now, you will never see the light of day again. You will wait in darkness and silence. You will be unable to move or speak ever again, until you stand before God to be sentenced to hell for eternity."

At that, I stood up right and waited a few moments. He continued to grimace and growl, but the spirit did not leave. Leaning forward, I whispered "Ok, you had your chance. Clearly, you didn't take me seriously. You think you are more powerful than me. Be you therefore an example, to all evil spirits, that I am who God says I am in Christ. My name is Ryker Ridge Kern, and in Jesus name I command you to be bound, gagged, and delivered into the pit until the day of your appointed judgment. You will never see the light of day again, nor will you ever harm anyone else for all eternity. I so command it now, in JESUS NAME!!!"

Suddenly, our friend let out a loud, fierce growl that extended for quite a bit. My wife said his face contorted into expressions of anger and rage, and he contorted dramatically in every direction before he fell completely limp. We maintained our positions for a few minutes, with no responsiveness in the man. He just hung limply in his chair. Finally, I leaned forward and spoke his name and asked, "Can you hear me?" He slurred a "Yes." So I said, "God wants some time with you. We are going to leave you here with Him. When you and God are done talking, come in the house. We will be waiting there." With that we got up and went inside. After that, this dear brother in the Lord was FREE, and changed.   His whole countenance was full of light, and he wasn't in bondage anymore.

Going after my stuff… "Where is my radio?"

One day, I took my daughter Sierra out on a hunting trip. When we got out to where we were going, she went in another direction with her Grandpa. I went in another with my brother. For safety purposes, I handed her a brand new two-way radio. I expressly looked her in the eye and said, "Don't lose this, it's expensive and brand new." She said she would take good care of it.

Later that day, we all gathered back again at the vehicles. I got there before her, but a few moments later she and my Dad came walking into camp. She had this sheepish look on her face and I asked her where the radio was. She said she had lost it somewhere up on the mountain but had no idea where it had fallen out of her pocket. I knew the general direction they had gone, but there was no trail and my Dad was way too tired to return to look for it.

So, I told her to grab her things because we were going back and looking for it until we found it. Try to imagine a young girl, who has never really been hunting like this before, trying to retrace her steps through miles of forest, brush, and rugged terrain. She had never been there before, and had only been following my Dad. She had no thought of having to remember where she had gone that day. Nevertheless, this is what she had to do. And, she had to find a little black radio smaller than the palm of her hand.

As we walked along, I told her we were not leaving without it. She must have thought I was nuts, and I can't say I'd blame her if she did. But the fact remained; it was unacceptable that we should ever lose anything again. God personally had told us we would never lose anything again, and we took Him at His Word. We would find it, and not stop until we did. So, we wandered through the thick brush and timber of this high alpine forest fruitlessly seeking the impossible.

I had no idea where they had gone. All I knew was their final destination. When we made it there we turned around and started walking back in the most likely path. There were many deer trails going in all directions. They most likely would follow one of those, but she had no idea which one. So, I started zigzagging across the ridges between the trails. Even as we were doing this, I realized how pointless it was. But, I was resolved. Standing in a thick patch of ferns, I said "Lord, I really want that radio back, can you please tell me where it is?" He replied, "Ryker, it's under that fern beside your left foot." I bent over, pushed the fern aside, and there on the ground in a clump of grass was the radio. "Whoa!!!

Getting our stuff back from the enemy... Belle's Brand New Camera

The radio story reminds me of another one. Some time ago, God told us we would never lose things again. Before this, Murphy's law had reigned in our life. It was pointless to have nice things. They either ended up broken, missing, or stolen. In this story, Belle had this new digital camera we had gotten her. It was somewhat expensive and she loved it. She was out with a friend one time, and when she got home the camera was missing. She recalled it had been in the top of her purse. She had hung the purse over the back of her chair at a restaurant. Then she recalled a suspicious looking man had been sitting behind her. He had been acting a little strangely, dancing in his chair, making noise and dropping things on the floor. All this, right around her purse.. She speculated that he may have stolen it there. I told her that people don't steal things from us anymore. So we searched the car and the house top to bottom, even though she had not seen it since the restaurant.

We searched for a couple of hours, believing in faith we would find it. As the search carried on I attempted to encourage her faith. She had vacuumed the car, and cleared all the counters until they were bare. I reminded her again that it would show up. God had promised us, and that was that. She remarked, "Does that mean if it was stolen, God will take it back and make it reappear here?" I said, "If necessary, yes." She replied, "I believe that".

With that, I stood up and headed to the car for another search there. Just as I walked past the bare cabinet next to the door, and took hold of the doorknob, Belle let out a shout. "There it is!!! I found my camera!!!" Sure enough, there it was lying on the cabinet I had just walked past, which she had cleared totally. Every flat surface in the house had already been cleared of everything during the search. Nevertheless, there was her camera!! In fact it was the only thing sitting on the cabinet. We were amazed. She had literally gone back to that cabinet many times, in the process. She just kept having this sense that it was there, even though there was nothing on the cabinet previously. "Whoa !!!"

Taking care of our animals... Chicken Little

Back at about the time of the missing radio, there was another event that most would not make much of. To us though, it was a cause for praise. We were just figuring out this thing about not losing things. The devil had taken so much from us over the years. We have lost everything on numerous occasions. God's promise that no more of this would occur, meant a great deal to us. Consequently, when even the smallest thing turned up missing, we were hypersensitive to it. Not because of the losses, as much as for the sake of the promise we were holding onto. We refused to tolerate any reality that contradicted God's promises.

For our daughters, we had some animals on our property. We had a horse, we had some bunny rabbits, and we had some chickens. This was our oldest daughter's "farmette" to take care of. Anyone who has ever kept small animals knows that their life expectancy is not that long. We had grown accustomed to the sad loss of our critters from time to time. It was just a fact of nature. However, we were in the process of measuring what were considered acceptable losses and what were not..

One night, a skunk broke into our hen house and made off with one of our hens. In my mind this constituted stealing. And it is the devil that comes to steal, kill, and destroy. Therefore, this was unacceptable. It made me angry. I was mad. I stomped out to the middle of our meadow, and shouted, "My name is Ryker Ridge Kern, and I declare in Jesus Name...YOU CANNOT HAVE MY CHICKEN !!! I WANT IT BACK AND I WANT IT BACK NOW !!!"

Anyone who has ever lost a chicken to skunks knows that they make short order of them. It was fairly certain, that by the time we discovered the chicken missing, it had already been eaten; and well what can you do then? I went back in the house and told my family to keep their eyes open for the missing chicken; she should be coming back anytime now. A couple hours later, our younger daughter, Savannah, came running back in the house with our little hen. The poor chicken was a little shaken up, had a few bloodied teeth marks, and some missing feathers, but despite her ordeal was none the worse for wear. We all laughed and rejoiced with our daughters. God is good, and to heck with the devil. We had our Chicken Little, and God's promise stood.

Defeating lies about ill health:

There was a time, when I had a strange pain in my abdomen. I tolerated it for over a year, praying it would go away. It never did though, and I started to realize maybe I was being foolish in not seeing a doctor. So, I went to the doctor and he did a bunch of tests. After the tests were done, he invited me to his office to go over the results. Looking me in the eye, he said, "I am sorry, but it appears that there is only one possible diagnosis that I can make. You have colon cancer." I was obviously startled by this, and asked him how he could be so sure. He went over the results of the various tests and explained what they meant. He then went on to give me all the information I needed about the specialist he was referring me to for further tests.

I was confused. Cancer cannot exist in my mortal body. God set me free of such things. I walked outside and sat in my car, taking in the news. I shook myself and then began to speak. I said, "Ok, I heard the doctor's report, and I know he is only doing his best for me. He only knows what he knows because of his training. But I have also had a lot of training and I have a report of my own. I am healthier than I have ever been, cancer cannot even exist in my mortal body. It is written, that disease cannot come near me, nor evil befall me, and I will have a long life (Psalms 91). Furthermore, I can only die of one thing and that is satisfaction. My hour has not come. It is written, "With a long life He will satisfy me, and then show me his salvation."

With that, I started the car and off I went into this adventure. As a wise steward, I let the doctors do their things. But for all their further tests, no evil disease was ever found. I was as healthy as could be. The pain in my abdomen? It disappeared after that. Whether cancer ever existed in my mortal body is a matter of debate. But here is what I do know: if I had received any of the doctor's reports, it would have existed in my mortal body. All it needed was my permission, whether by consent or deceit, it made no difference. Disease came knocking on my door that day and I told it where to go.

Getting rid of Scar Tissue:

This cancer report reminds me of another similar situation that was even more impressive. Years ago, long before we understood these principles and had been delivered from our impotent doctrines, we had a scary experience. In one of Belle's checkups, with the doctor, they informed her she had cervical dysplasia. Apparently, this is considered precancerous cells that dangerously often result in cancer. They said it was ok though, because it was caught in time to treat with laser surgery. We opted to have the surgery. The final report, afterwards, was that it was a successful operation. In the years to come, the doctors would always watch her closely to make sure it did not come back. They always noted in their reports about the scar tissue left from the surgery, for there was more than usual... there was an inch long deeper scar that had been left. Many years later, after we had learned the spiritual truths we know now, her doctors gave her some bad news again. Apparently, the dysplasia was back, only this time it was more severe, and she needed to get into surgery immediately.

At this point, we did understand about walking in faith but were still very new to it. Such news can rock one's world. But it didn't. We stood on the promises of God and we gave our own report on the matter. A few days later, she was scheduled to meet the surgeon who was going to do his pre-surgery assessment. That morning, she asked me to pray for her, which I did. Then I said, "Sweetheart, this is how your day is going to go. When the surgeon does his assessment today, he is not going to find anything to do surgery on. He will tell you your cervix is perfectly healthy and he is not going to have any idea what this other doctor was talking about. Watch and see, My Love...it's going to be a good day."

After she got out, I asked her, "So, what did the doctor say?" She said, "It was the strangest thing. He kept looking through his scope and back at his report for an odd amount of time and kept muttering something to himself. I began to be concerned, and asked if everything was ok. He stood up, and said "I have no idea what this other doctor is talking about, your cervix is perfectly healthy. There is nothing wrong with you." Astonished, she asked, "Can you please check one more time? In my file it says there is a deep scar, from the previous surgery. You do at least see that, right?" He agreed to check again, and note the scar on the records too. After checking once more, He said "I'm sorry, but despite what this report says, your cervix is perfectly healthy and if there ever was any scar tissue, it's gone now." "Whoa!!!"

You and I both know scar tissue never goes away. And cancer does not just disappear in the matter of moments. Well, in the natural world anyway. But in the Kingdom of Heaven, anything that contradicts the Word of God concerning us does. It is therefore not difficult for me to choose Whom to serve and to which kingdom I will submit to.

There are many, many more such stories that exist, as standing stones in our lives. Long ago, I began a list. I called it my "Red Sea list." It is a list of miracles we have had in our lives or witnessed in others. I kept it up for a long time. But like so many things, it gotten to be too labor intensive to keep up. The miracles happened so frequently, that I just quit keeping track of them. At one point, I became concerned about it and started recording a series called "The things I have seen and heard." Then that got to be so much that I eventually dropped this project too. Here is what I know. People who expect miracles, often get far more than they bargained for. People who expect miracles, get an amazing life.

A New Backbone

CONCLUSION – VOLUME ONE

So, we come to the conclusion of volume one. It would be preferable to look at this as an intermission, however. In volume one, we have come a long ways together. Half the story is like half of anything though. It is incomplete. For the most part, volume one covered a time of unlearning and reconstruction. Volume two takes us into the most dramatic and intense visions so far. Ultimately though, volume two takes us where volume one was going. Without moving on, it is as in life; we never arrive.

Following is a chapter by chapter summary of what one will find ahead in volume two.

Secret Place Visions
Volume Two Summary

Chapter One: Blessings for My Belle

After stripping paint from the outside walls for a little while, Jesus invited me inside for a glass of ice tea. As we sipped our tea, we discussed plans for the chapel's renovation. In particular, we discussed the construction of a bell tower and the installation of a bell. Before leaving, He pours out blessings for my wife, Belle.

Chapter Two: Golden Belle

The next time I opened my eyes in a vision, I was standing at the head of the path to the chapel. This time however, someone had come and bulldozed a fresh road bed to it. Walking into the clearing I noted stacks of building supplies, and in particular one large crate. Inside the crate was a beautiful solid gold bell for the tower. We further discussed renovation plans. Before letting me go, He mentioned that it would be possible for me to drive to the chapel next time.

Chapter Three: Blue Prints

This time, I drove to the chapel. Upon parking, I noted that there were two men repairing the roof. A closer look revealed them to be the two most influential men in my life. After some discussion, I presented Jesus with my proposed blue prints for the renovation.

Chapter Four: Krista

During a time of severe spiritual attack, I found it almost impossible to enter into my secret place. At a time when I needed it the most it became virtually inaccessible. Finally, one day I made it and there found counsel from the Lord. During our conversation, much to my astonishment, we received our first visitor in the "The Secret Place." A very emotional reception followed.

Chapter Five: You Are Not My God!!!

As a result of ongoing spiritual attacks, accessing my "Secret Place" continued to be difficult, if not impossible. After many attempts, I finally succeeded only to find that it appeared as if my "Secret Place" had been the battlefield for a hostile attack. Everything that had been accomplished so far, had been utterly destroyed. Upon entering what was left of the structure I was greeted by the Lord. However, amidst our discussion, I realized that this was not the Lord at all, but rather the devil himself masquerading as Jesus. After driving Him out, Jesus appears and taking me in an embrace, ministers to me. Following Him outside, He shows me that all the debris from the attack is being picked up by people I was familiar with. Then, taking me up in the air above my "Secret Place," He showed me many other similar secret places off in the distance and encouraged me to know that we are not alone.

Chapter Six: Martha

The next time my eyes opened on this place, a great deal had changed. The bell tower was nearly finished, and someone was preparing to hoist the Golden Belle into the tower. Inside, Jesus greeted me and showed off the polished new hardwood floors. Leading me to a particular Enclave, He opened its door and had me stand in the light which poured out from it. While He tended to other matters, I continued to stand in the light. As I waited for Him to return, the next visitor came to my "Secret Place." In an amusing conversation, we both enjoy the light. When Jesus returned He spent some quality time with my visitor.

Chapter Seven: Words of Freedom

Walking into the chapel now, I find it nearing completion. This time it is also filled with beautiful new pews. As we talk, people start coming in and seating themselves. Jesus informs me that they are going to want to hear a word from me. He asks what I intend to say. We discuss the first and foremost lesson to dedicate this chapel in the woods.

Chapter Eight: The Book of Days

Leaning on a plain unadorned Enclave in the shadows of a corner, Jesus asks me if I remember where He found me. He reminds me of a moment in the past. Then, He opens the Enclave and presents me with large leather bound book. Using a key He had given me, I opened a lock that secured the book closed. Turning to the first page I read the title: "The Book of Days."

Chapter Nine: The Book of Days - Title Page

Wanting to know more about "The Book of Days," Jesus grants my request to see it again. Reading the first page once more, I read the title "The Book of Days." Underneath this title though were these words in a smaller font. "The Exploits of the Great Kings in the Last Days." Seated on the sofa in my study, Jesus explained the nature of this intriguing book.

Chapter Ten: The Book of Days – Introduction

Hungry to know more, Jesus lets me look at the book one more time. This time, I read the introduction page to "The Book of Days." Reading it provided an inspiring glimpse into the future.

An Invitation to Ask Questions and

Share your Thoughts

After reading this book, you may have questions, have been inspired to recall a story or vision of your own, or possibly have a testimony to share. If so, we would love to hear from you. As you might imagine we are pretty busy so while a phone call may be difficult, we always reply to e-mails. If you would like information about the books to follow this or would like to schedule Ryker for a speaking engagement you may also contact us via e-mail.

Ryker and Belle Kern

73858 Valle Vista Rd.

Twentynine Palms, CA 92277

www.northgate29@gmail.com